Let's Bread!

The Bread Machine Cookbook for Beginners

THE
COOKBOOKS LAB
BY ANDROMEDA PUBLISHING

D1672108

Table of Content

Introduction

...... Crusty outside, soft inside and a smell that cannot be confused with anything else in the world...so. Who doesn't love freshly baked bread!?!?

It gives me goosebumps every time I meet it, it delivers such a nostalgic feeling: all the way from my mom's home-baked golden bricks to my current hobby. In its notes there's past, there's present, and there's definitely future!

These warm sentiments and my understanding of the importance are probably the main reasons for this book, as in culinary there's nothing more essential than bread, and making it is real science. Bread is the culmination of all our hours of work and waiting. Baking day is like science-fair day, Feast Day, and Judgment Day, all making a love child together.

...I presume you want to start baking too! That sounds like music to my truly bread-loving ears, and I really want to help you start! Bread baking is not hard per se, but can indeed be intimidating. We've all been there at the start, and, from experience, I can tell you that it's easier than you think.

Even if you have never unwrapped a package of yeast or taken your dough hook out of the box, don't worry about a thing - with my help you've got this. I tried my best to answer all your questions and give you the best advice in this book, making your way as easy as possible.

Baking Using a Bread Machine

A bread maker machine contains a few basic parts. In simple terms, you can think of a bread machine as a tiny oven, the size of a loaf of bread. It will have a built-in pan that will be your only available bread or dough size, and some sort of electronic dial to operate it. The other most important part is that your machine will probably have a removable paddle that you can attach to the pan; this paddle serves to stir up the ingredients and create your dough for you.

It mixes, kneads, proofs, and bakes bread – all at the push of a button. Of all the many different ways machines can make our lives easier, taking the hard work out of baking bread has to rank way up there among the all-time greats.

But how exactly do you bake using a bread machine?

All bread maker varieties will be slightly different, and how you use it will be up to the particular instructions for your machine. There are some common steps that you will probably take no matter which bread machine you have, but always read your instruction manual for specifics. The first step, of course, will be mixing in all the different ingredients.

When you make bread by hand, you combine the ingredients very carefully and in a specific order - this does not change when you use a bread machine. Every machine has a different order of ingredients listed, but most will be compiled of the following essential ingredients:

- 1 cup warm water
- 2 tsp Sugar
- 2 tsp Salt
- 4 cups flour, sifted
- 2½ tsp active dry yeast
- 2 tsp oil

Once you have added all of the correct ingredients, you should set the bread machine to whatever setting is recommended for your desired bread type. The instruction manual and recipes included in the machine should have some suggestions as to which settings work best for which types of bread.

After you set it, the paddle attachment that we talked about earlier will mix and knead your ingredients into the perfect bread dough! Then you will need to complete another step - you will need to set your bread machine to the right baking settings. Some machines can do this step from the beginning as well, but most will require you to do something between the mixing and the baking stages.

Many modern bread machines have timers on them so that you can mix the dough and then set it not to bake until later on. Imagine setting it so that you wake up to a freshly baked bread loaf in the morning! But whether or not your machine has a timer, it will cook your single loaf of bread for the perfect amount of time for your desired setting.

Usually, the bread machine bakes a loaf of bread in around three to four hours. There have been quicker models released in recent years that can bake an entire loaf in under an hour. The benefit, either way, is that you do not need to stay up to take the bread out of the oven and turn off the oven. The sub-hour breads typically are not quite as high quality as those that are allowed the full normal baking time, but we understand that sometimes you're in a pinch!

There you have it: three simple steps to creating delicious homemade bread with your bread machine. The process is so much easier than making your bread by hand that you will not regret this investment! Your friends and family will be all too happy to help taste test all of your yummy new creations.

Settings

If you are not quite sure about what all the cycles and settings of your exact machine are, and you don't have a user manual, or you bought the machine second-hand, this subchapter will help you to understand the basics. It will also help you to select the correct cycle if the recipe that you want to use does not specify which you should use. The most common bread machine settings and cycles are explained here for quick reference.

Basic

Ideal for basic bread, made in the American style, this setting is excellent for most savory yeast bread. It's important not to use this cycle for sweet yeast breads accidentally, as you can overprove your loaf, doing so.

Sweet

Most bread maker's sweet cycle is to prepare and bake sweet yeast bread. However, don't get it confused with the quick bread cycle, as quick breads do not contain yeast, therefore they cook at a different pace and require no rise time.

Whole Wheat

Whole wheat flour takes a bit longer to make decent bread, as for the gluten to get to work the rise time is generally longer in this cycle. Some bakers gateway-choose to add wheat gluten to whole wheat loaves, which may allow the basic cycle to be used. That said, for stable results, stick with the intended whole wheat setting.

French

The French setting isn't exclusively for French bread! Many European style breads, specifically originating from Western Europe, will do better on this setting. The timing here is a bit longer than on the basic loaf cycle, and temperature settings may also differ.

Gluten-Free

Individuals with special diets and preferences may require gluten- free bakery, so bread makers often include a very special cycle for gluten-free bread to help these individuals. In general, gluten-free bread ingredients advise using room temperature ingredients and flours like millet, almond, or sorghum.

Quick/Rapid

Sometimes named a fast cycle, and other times named rapid, this cycle is for baking in a hurry. This cycle differs from one machine to another, but in general, implies speeding up the rising times. In some machines, special rapid rise yeast may be required for this cycle.

Quick Bread

This is the cycle you will get the most use out of if you adore and bake banana nut bread and similar treats. It is intended for use with quick bread recipes, quick bread, as a rule, can be baked immediately – it requires little to no rise time.

Dough

The dough cycle is excellent for making bread dough when you want to form the loaves yourself. It saves you from quite a lot of mess and work since it does all the kneading and mixing for you. It works really well with the timer, so you can set the dough to be ready when you are ready to shape it into rolls or a loaf and bake it.

Other/Custom

Some machines offer users the possibility to create their own cycles, set the time when the cycle will begin, bake for preset times, or perform other advanced options. This will give you the ultimate control to get your perfect loaf.

If you are unsure about the function of one of your bread machine's cycles, you can always test it on an empty loaf pan, with the paddle in place. It should be relatively easy to tell what is going on during the cycle, even with no dough in the machine. For a better view, open the lid. You won't damage the machine in the process, so don't worry.

So, as shown, bread machine cycles and settings are easy enough to use once you are familiarized with your machine.

The Right Bread Machine

The good bread makers are all relatively simple devices that mostly follow the same lines and build on simple principles.

The real value of bread makers is that they allow you to create almost any type of bread you can think of.

With almost each bread maker, you will get essential measuring devices and a bread pan into which the ingredients go.

There'll also be a series of control buttons on the machine, which allow you to switch the settings to bake the bread you want (white, brown, French, etc.).

Many of the bigger machines also allow you to make loaves of different sizes (large, medium, small). All, of course, have timers, so you can make sure you wake up or return from work to a fresh warm bread if you like. Kneading is done by a paddle, which stays in during the baking (and often, on lesser machines, gets lodged into the end product, meaning you have to hook it out – hook provided).

But there are many other important variables to consider, and here is the list.

Bread Maker Size

Smaller bread makers produce tall, square-shaped loaves, while the ones that bake traditional "horizontal" loaves take up a little more space on your kitchen counter.

The size of a bread machine also directly relates to the size of the loaf it can bake. Consider your regular needs before making a choice, since a one-pound loaf will be perfect for a small family dinner (with some likely leftover for lunch), but for a dinner party, you'll need at least one 2 pounder.

One Paddle or Two

Some machines only have one paddle for kneading, others have two. The dual paddle solution is more expensive and kneads horizontal loaves much better, while a single paddle is usually fine for vertical and small horizontal loaves. There are also models with collapsible or removable paddles, which don't leave the hole from the paddle in the underside of a loaf.

Varieties of Loaves Available

You'll need to take a look at each model to see what loaves it can bake. They all have a different set of pre-programmed settings, and often you may not find all of your favorites available at once. For instance, ensure that the breadmaker has a "gluten-free" or "rye" setting if those are a must for you. Most machines let you choose whether you want a dark, medium, or light level of crust, so that shouldn't be an issue.

Complicated Fruit Breads

Low-end bread makers aren't the best choice for those who want to make bread with nuts or dried fruit inside, because the ingredients will be chopped into little pieces by the paddles at the very beginning of the process. If done properly, they need to be added partway through baking, so you'll need a model with an automatic dispenser that will add the nuts and fruits at the right time or at least the one that signals you to manually add the ingredients.

Want to Make More Than Bread?

Some bread makers offer the ability to make more than just bread. Knead-only settings allow you to make great pasta and pizza dough, machines with bake-only settings are perfect for fruitcake or gingerbread, and some also let you bake regular cakes or make jams and jellies.

Extra Features – Quick Bake, Timers and Windows

One feature often found on bread makers is a godsend for some people and useless for others. It's the "quick bake" setting that lets you bake a loaf of bread in an hour or even less, and many with hectic lives absolutely love it. Be aware, though, that the quality of the bread produced will be noticeably lower than if the loaf had its normal three or four hours to bake.

White Bread Recipes

1.Basic White Bread

Servings: **16 slices**   Prep Time: **6 min.**   Cook Time: **2.50 h**

Ingredients

- *1 cup warm water (about 110°F/45°C)*
- *2 Tbsp sugar*
- *2¼ tsp (.25-ounce package) bread machine yeast*
- *¼ cup rice bran oil*
- *3 cups bread flour*
- *1 tsp salt*

Carbs **18 g**   Fat **1 g**   Protein **3 g**   Calories **95**

Directions

- *Add each ingredient to the bread machine in the order and at the temperature recommended by your bread machine manufacturer.*
- *Close the lid, select the basic or white bread, low crust setting on your bread machine, and press start.*

- *When the bread machine has finished baking, remove the bread and put it on a cooling rack.*

2. *Extra Buttery White Bread*

Servings: **16 slices**   *Prep Time:* **11 min.**   *Cook Time:* **3 h. 10 min.**

Ingredients

- *1⅛ cups milk*
- *4 Tbsp unsalted butter*
- *3 cups bread flour*
- *½ Tbsp white granulated sugar*
- *1½ tsp salt*
- *1½ tsp bread machine yeast*

Carbs **22 g**   *Fat* **1 g**   *Protein* **4 g**   *Calories* **04**

Directions

- *Soften the butter in your microwave.*
- *Add each ingredient to the bread machine in the order and at the temperature recommended by your bread machine manufacturer.*
- *Close the lid, select the basic or white bread, medium crust setting on your bread machine, and press start.*

- *the bread machine has finished baking, remove the bread and put it on a cooling rack.*

3. Mom's White Bread

Servings: **16 slices**   Prep Time: **5 min.**   Cook Time: **3 h.**

Ingredients

- 1 cup and 3 Tbsp water
- 2 Tbsp vegetable oil
- 1½ tsp salt
- 2 Tbsp sugar
- 3¼ cups white bread flour
- 2 tspcive dry yeast

Carbs **17 g**   Fat **1 g**   Protein **3 g**   Calories **90**

Directions

- *Add each ingredient to the bread machine in the order and at the temperature recommended by your bread machine manufacturer.*
- *Close the lid, select the basic or white bread, medium crust setting on your bread machine, and press start.*
- *When the bread machine has finished baking, remove the bread and put it on a cooling rack.*

4. Vegan White Bread

Servings: 14 slices **Prep Time:** 5 min. **Cook Time:** 3 h.

Ingredients

- ⅓ cups water
- ⅓ cup plant milk (soy milk its ok)
- 1½ tsp salt
- 2 Tbsp granulated sugar
- 2 Tbsp vegetable oil
- 3½ cups all-purpose flour
- 1¾ tsp bread machine yeast

Carbs 13 g   **Fat** 2 g   **Protein** 3 g   **Calories** 80

Directions

- Add each ingredient to the bread machine in the order and at the temperature recommended by your bread machine manufacturer.
- Close the lid, select the basic or white bread, medium crust setting on your bread machine, and press start.
- When the bread machine has finished baking, remove the bread and put it on a cooling rack

5. Rice Flour Rice Bread

Servings: **16 slices**	Prep Time: **10 min.**	Cook Time: **3 h.15 min.**

Ingredients

- 3 eggs
- 1½ cups water
- 3 Tbsp vegetable oil
- 1 tsp apple cider vinegar
- 2¼ tsp active dry yeast
- 3¼ cups white rice flour
- 2½ tsp xanthan gum
- 1½ tsp salt
- ½ cup dry milk powder
- 3 Tbsp white sugar

Carbs **24 g**	Fat **1 g**	Protein **2 g**	Calories **110**

Directions

- In a medium-size bowl, mix the eggs, water, oil, and vinegar.
- In a large bowl, add the yeast, salt, xanthan gum, dry milk powder, rice flour, and sugar. Mix with a whisk until incorporated.
- Add each ingredient to the bread machine in the order and at the temperature recommended by your bread machine manufacturer.
- Close the lid, select the whole wheat, medium crust setting on your bread machine, and press start.

- *When the bread machine has finished baking, remove the bread and put it on a cooling rack.*

6. Italian White Bread

Servings: **14 slices**   Prep Time: **5 min.**   Cook Time: **3 h.**

Ingredients

- ¾ cup cold water
- 2 cups bread flour
- 1 Tbsp sugar
- 1 tsp salt
- 1 Tbsp olive oil
- tsp active dry yeast

Carbs **11 g**   Fat **1 g**   Protein **2 g**   Calories **78**

Directions

- *Add each ingredient to the bread machine in the order and at the temperature recommended by your bread machine manufacturer.*
- *Close the lid, select the Italian or basic bread, low crust setting on your bread machine, and press start.*

- *When the bread machine has finished baking, remove the bread and put it on a cooling rack.*

7.Anadama White Bread

Servings: **14 Slices**   *Prep Time:* **5 Min.**   *Cook Time:* **3 h.**

Ingredients

- *1⅛ cups water (110°F/43°C)*
- *⅓ cup molasses*
- *1½ Tbsp butter at room temperature*
- *1 tsp salt*
- *⅓ cup yellow cornmeal*
- *3½ cups bread flour*
- *2½ tsp bread machine yeast*

Carbs **19 g**   *Fat* **1 g**   *Protein* **2 g**   *Calories* **96**

Directions

- *Add each ingredient to the bread machine in the order and at the temperature recommended by your bread machine manufacturer.*
- *Close the lid, select the basic bread, low crust setting on your bread machine, and press start.*

- *When the bread machine has finished baking, remove the bread and put it on a cooling rack.*

8. Soft White Bread

Servings: **14 Slices**   Prep Time: **5 Min.**   Cook Time: **3 h**

Ingredients

- *2 cups water*
- *4 tsp yeast*
- *6 Tbsp sugar*
- *½ cup vegetable oil*
- *2 tsp salt*
- *3 cups strong white flour*

Carbs **18 g**   Fat **1 g**   Protein **4 g**   Calories **93**

Directions

- *Add each ingredient to the bread machine in the order and at the temperature recommended by your bread machine manufacturer.*
- *Close the lid, select the basic bread, low crust setting on your bread machine, and press start.*

- *When the bread machine has finished baking, remove the bread and put it on a cooling rack.*

Did You Know?

1) Sliced bread was only invented in 1928 and was referred to as the best thing since bagged bread.

2) In WWII, rationing laws prohibited the sale of freshly-baked bread because "the tastiness of just-baked bread is likely to encourage people to eat it immoderately". The bread had to be at least 24 hours old before it was sold

3) The yeast we use to make bread is an organism floating around in the air we breathe. Anyone can capture it easily.

4) The distinction of "upper crust" comes from the 1600s. When the bread was made in stone ovens the bottoms would become dirty from ash and soot. If you were wealthy you cut the bottom crust off and just ate the "upper crust" part of the bread.

5) Feeding bread to ducks actually causes many health problems for them.

BREAKFAST

BREADS

9. English Muffin Bread

Ingredients

- *1 tsp vinegar*
- *¼ to ⅓ cup water*
- *1 cup lukewarm milk*
- *2 Tbsp butter or 2 Tbsp vegetable oil*
- *1½ tsp salt*
- *1½ tsp sugar*
- *½ tsp baking powder*
- *3½ cups unbleached all-purpose flour*
- *2¼ tsp instant yeast*

Carbs **13 g**   *Fat* **1 g**   *Protein* **2 g**   *Calories* **62**

Directions

- *Add each ingredient to the bread machine in the order and at the temperature recommended by your bread machine manufacturer.*
- *Close the lid, select the basic bread, low crust setting on your bread machine, and press start.*
- *3When the bread machine* has finished baking, remove the bread and put it on a cooling rack.

10. Cranberry Orange Breakfast Bread

Ingredients

- 1⅛ cup orange juice
- 2 Tbsp vegetable oil
- 2 Tbsp honey
- 3cups bread flour
- 1 Tbsp dry milk powder
- ½ tsp ground cinnamon
- ½ tsp ground allspice 1 tsp salt
- 1 (.25 ounce) package active dry yeast
- 1 Tbsp grated orange zest
- 1 cup sweetened dried cranberries
- ⅓ cup chopped walnuts

Carbs **29 g**   Fat **2 g**   Protein **5 g**   Calories **160**

Directions

- 1.Add each ingredient to the bread machine in the order and at the temperature recommended by your bread machine manufacturer.
- Close the lid, select the basic bread, low crust setting on your bread machine, and press start.
- Add the cranberries and chopped walnuts 5 to 10 minutes before last kneading cycle ends.

- *When the bread machine has finished baking, remove the bread and put it on a cooling rack.*

11. Buttermilk Honey Bread

Servings: **14 slices**   *Prep Time:* **5 min.**   *Cook Time:* **3 h. 35 min.**

Ingredients

- ½ cup water
- ¾ cup buttermilk
- ¼ cup honey
- 3 Tbsp butter, softened   cut into pieces
- 3 cups bread flour
- 1½ tsp salt
- 2¼ tsp yeast (or 1 package)

Carbs **19 g**   *Fat* **1 g**   *Protein* **2 g**   *Calories* **92**

Directions

- *Add each ingredient to the bread machine in the order and at the temperature recommended by your bread machine manufacturer.*
- *Close the lid, select the basic bread, medium crust setting on your bread machine and press start.*
- *When the bread machine has finished baking, remove the bread and put it on a cooling rack.*

12. Whole Wheat Breakfast Bread

Servings: **14 slices**   Prep Time: **5 min.**   Cook Time: **3 h**

Ingredients

- **3 cups white whole wheat flour**
- **½ tsp salt**
- **1 cup water**
- **½ cup coconut oil, liquified 4 Tbsp honey**
- **2½ tsp active dry yeast**

Carbs **11 g**   Fat **3 g**   Protein **1 g**   Calories **60**

Directions

- *Add each ingredient to the bread machine in the order and at the temperature recommended by your bread machine manufacturer.*
- *Close the lid, select the basic bread, medium crust setting on your bread machine and press start.*

- *When the bread machine has finished baking, remove the bread and put it on a cooling rack.*

13. Raisin Bread

Servings: 14 slices   Prep Time: 5 min.   Cook Time: 3 h.30 min.

Ingredients

- *1cup water*
- *2Tbsp butter, softened*
- *3cups Gold Medal Better for Bread flour*
- *3 Tbsp sugar*
- *1½ tsp salt*
- *1 tsp ground cinnamon*
- *2½ tsp bread machine yeast*
- *¾ cup raisins*

Carbs **38 g**   Fat **2 g**   Protein **4 g**   Calories **180**

Directions

- *Add each ingredient except the raisins to the bread machine in the order and at the temperature recommended by your bread machine manufacturer.*
- *Close the lid, select the sweet or basic bread, medium crust setting on your bread machine and press start.*

- Add raisins 10 minutes before the last kneading cycle ends.
- When the bread machine has finished baking, remove the bread and put it on a cooling rack.

14. Banana Bread

Servings: *14 Slices*   Prep Time: *5 Min.*   Cook Time: *3 H. 15 Min.*

Ingredients

- 1½ cups bread flour
- ⅔ cup sugar
- 1 tsp baking powder
- ½ tsp baking soda
- ½ tsp salt
- ⅓ cup butter, melted
- 2 large eggs, lightly beaten
- 1 tsp vanilla
- ⅔ cup mashed banana/milk

Carbs *32 g*   Fat *7 g*   Protein *3 g*   Calories *190*

Directions

- Add each ingredient to the bread machine in the order and at the temperature recommended by your bread machine manufacturer.

- *Close the lid, select the sweet or basic bread, medium crust setting on your bread machine and press start.*
- *When the bread machine has finished baking, remove the bread and put it on a cooling rack.*

15. Cranberry & Golden Raisin Bread

Servings: **14 Slices**   *Prep Time:* **5 Min.**   *Cook Time:* **3 H.**

Ingredients

- *1 ⅓ cups water*
- *4 Tbsp sliced butter 3 cups flour*
- *1 cup old fashioned oatmeal*
- *⅓ cup brown sugar 1 tsp salt*
- *4 Tbsp dried cranberries 4 Tbsp golden raisins*
- *2 tsp bread machine yeast*

Carbs **33 g**   *Fat* **3 g**   *Protein* **4 g**   *Calories* **175**

Directions

- *Add each ingredient except cranberries and golden raisins to the bread machine one by one, according to the manufacturer's instructions.*

- *Close the lid, select the sweet or basic bread, medium crust setting on your bread machine and press start.*
- *Add the cranberries and golden raisins 5 to 10 minutes before the last kneading cycle ends.*
- *When the bread machine has finished baking, remove the bread and put it on a cooling rack.*

SANDWICH BREAD

16. Soft Sandwich Bread

Servings: *14 slices*   **Prep Time:** *5 min.*   **Cook Time:** *3 h.*

Ingredients

- 2 Tbsp sugar
- 1 cup water
- 1 Tbsp yeast
- ¼ cup vegetable oil
- 3 cups white flour
- 2 tsp salt

Carbs – *32 g*   **Fat** – *1 g*   **Protein** – *6 g*   **Calories** – *169*

Directions

- *Add each ingredient to the bread machine in the order and at the temperature recommended by your bread machine manufacturer.*
- *Close the lid, select the basic bread, low crust setting on your bread machine and press start.*
- *When the bread machine has finished baking, remove the bread and put it on a cooling rack.*

17 Hawaiian Sandwich Bread

Servings: *14 Slices*   **Prep Time:** *5 Min.*   **Cook Time:** *3 H.*

Ingredients

- ¾ cup pineapple juice
1egg
- 2½ Tbsp olive oil
- 4 level Tbsp sugar
- 1 tsp kosher salt
- 3 level cups breadflour
- ½ cup milk
- 2 level tsp quick rise yeast

Carbs – *21 g*   **Fat** – *3 g*   **Protein** – *3 g*   **Calories** – *120*

Directions

- Add each ingredient to the bread machine in the order and at the temperature recommended by your bread machine manufacturer.

- *Close the lid, select the basic bread, low crust setting on your bread machine and press start.*
- *When the bread machine has finished baking, remove the bread and put it on a cooling rack.*

18 Gluten-Free White Bread

Servings: **14 Slices**   Prep Time: **5 Min.**   Cook Time: **3 H.**

Ingredients

- *2 eggs*
- *1 ⅓ cups milk*
- *6 Tbsp oil*
- *tsp vinegar*
- *3⅝ cups white bread flour 1*
- *tsp salt*
- *2Tbsp sugar*
- *2 tsp dove farm quick yeast*

Carbs – *18 g*   Fat – *3 g*   Protein – *2 g*   Calories – *90*

Directions

- *Add each ingredient to the bread machine in the order and at the temperature recommended by your bread machine manufacturer.*
- *Close the lid and start the machine on the gluten free bread program, if available. Alternatively use the basic or rapid setting with a dark crust option.*
- *When the bread machine has finished baking, remove the bread and put it on a cooling rack.*

19 Honey Whole-Wheat Sandwich Bread

Servings: 14 Slices   *Prep Time: 5 Min.*   *Cook Time: 3 H*

Ingredients

- 4¼ cups whole-wheat flour
- ½ tsp salt
- 1½ cups water
- ¼ cup honey
- 2 Tbsp olive oil, or melted butter
- 2¼ tsp bread machine yeast (1 packet)

Carbs – 36 g   *Fat – 3 g*   *Protein – 6 g*   *Calories – 190*

Directions

- Add each ingredient to the bread machine in the order and at the temperature recommended by your bread machine manufacturer.
- Close the lid, select the whole wheat, low crust setting on your bread machine and press start.
- When the bread machine has finished baking, remove the bread and put it on a cooling rack.

Did You Know?

6) Bread goes stale 6x faster in the fridge than at room temperature.

7) Ancient Egyptians used moldy bread as a treatment for infected burn wounds, possibly already utilizing the antibiotic effects of molds accidentally discovered by Alexander Fleming.

8) In France, by law a bakery has to make all the bread it sells from scratch in order to have the right to be called a baker

9) Cinnamon can prevent mold growth. Scientists have created cinnamon-based packaging that can prevent mold in bread in other baked goods.

10) Nearly all the bread clips, those flat, U-shaped pieces of plastic are produced by one family-owned company in Yakima, Washington. The first one was carved from a credit card, the company exports billions a year, and the Kwik Lok Corporation has an almost complete monopoly.

11) The Boudin Bakery in San Francisco has been making sourdough bread for 166 years and every loaf of sourdough bread they make has a portion of the original "mother dough" from 1849 in it

SAVORY BREADS SPICE AND HERB BREADS

20 Italian Herb Bread

Ingredients

- *2 Tbsp margarine*
- *2 Tbsp sugar*
- *1½ cups water*
- *3 Tbsp powdered milk*
- *1½ tsp dried marjoram*
- *1½ tsp dried basil*
- *1½ tsp salt*
- *4 cups bread flour*
- *1¼ tsp yeast*
- *1½ tsp dried thyme*

Carbs – **20 g**   *Fat* – **3 g**   *Protein* – **4 g**   *Calories* – **120**

Directions

- *Add each ingredient to the bread machine in the order and at the temperature recommended by your bread machine manufacturer.*
- *Close the lid, select the basic bread, medium crust setting on your bread machine, and press start.*
- *When the bread machine has finished baking, remove the bread and put it on a cooling rack.*

21 Caramelized *Onion Bread*

Servings: *14 Slices*   Prep Time: *15 Min.*   Cook Time: *3 H.35 Min.*

Ingredients

- ½ Tbsp butter
- ½ cup onions, sliced
- 1 cup water
- 1 Tbsp olive oil
- 3 cups Gold Medal Better for Bread flour
- 2 Tbsp sugar
- 1 tsp salt
- 1¼ tsp bread machine or quick active dry yeast

Carbs – *30 g*   Fat – *3 g*   Protein – *4 g*   Calories – *160*

Directions

- Melt the butter over medium-low heat in a skillet.
- Cook the onions in the butter for 10 to 15 minutes until they are brown and caramelized - then remove from the heat.
- Add each ingredient except the onions to the bread machine in the order and at the temperature recommended by your bread machine manufacturer.
- Close the lid, select the basic bread, medium crust setting on your bread machine and press start.

- Add ½ cup of onions 5 to 10 minutes before the last kneading cycle ends.
- When the bread machine has finished baking, remove the bread and put it on a cooling rack.

22 Olive Bread

Servings: 14 Slices **Prep Time:** 10 Min. **Cook Time:** 3 H.

Ingredients

- ½ cup brine from olive jar
- Add warm water (110°F) To make 1½ cup when combined with brine
- 2 Tbsp olive oil
- 3 cups bread flour
- ⅔ cups whole wheat flour
- 1½ tsp salt
- 2 Tbsp sugar
- 1½ tsp dried leaf basil
- 2 tsp active dry yeast
- ⅔ cup finely chopped Kalamata olives

Carbs – 28 g   Fat – 1 g   Protein – 5 g   Calories – 140

Directions

- Add each ingredient except the olives to the bread machine in the order and at the temperature recommended by your bread machine manufacturer.

- *Close the lid, select the wheat, medium crust setting on your bread machine and press start.*
- *Add the olives 10 minutes before the last kneading cycle ends.*
- *When the bread machine has finished baking, remove the bread and put it on a cooling rack.*

23 Dilly Onion Bread

Servings: **14** Slices   Prep Time: **10 Min.**   Cook Time: **3 H.5 Min.**

Ingredients

- ¾ *cup water (70°F to 80°F)*
- *1 Tbsp butter, softened*
- *2 Tbsp sugar*
- *3 Tbsp dried minced onion*
- *2 Tbsp dried parsley flakes*
- *1 Tbsp dill weed*
- *1 tsp salt*
- *1 garlic clove, minced*

- *2 cups bread flour*
- ⅓ *cup whole wheat flour*
- *Tbsp nonfat dry milk powder*
- *2 tsp active dry yeast serving*

Carbs – **16 g**   Fat – **1 g**   Protein – **3 g**   Calories – **77**

Directions

- *Add each ingredient to the bread machine in the order and at the temperature recommended by your bread machine manufacturer.*
- *Close the lid, select the basic bread, medium crust setting on your bread machine and press start.*
- *When the bread machine has finished baking, remove the bread and put it on a cooling rack.*

24. Cardamom Cranberry Bread

Servings: *14 Slices* Prep Time: *5 Min.* Cook Time: *3 H.*

Ingredients

- 1¾ cups water
- 2 Tbsp brown sugar
- 1½ tsp salt
- 2 Tbsp coconut oil
- 4 cups flour
- 2 tsp cinnamon
- 2 tsp cardamom
- 1 cup dried cranberries
- 2 tsp yeast

Carbs – *41 g* Fat – *3 g* Protein – *3 g* Calories – *157*

Directions

- Add each ingredient except the dried cranberries to the bread machine in the order and at the temperature recommended by your bread machine manufacturer.
- Close the lid, select the basic bread, medium crust setting on your bread machine and press start.
- Add the dried cranberries 5 to 10 minutes before the last kneading cycle ends.
- When the bread machine has finished baking, remove the bread and put it on a cooling rack.

25 Rosemary Bread

Servings: *14 Slices*   **Prep Time:** *5 Min.*   **Cook Time:** *3 H.*

Ingredients

- 1 ⅓ cups milk
- 4 Tbsp butter
- 3 cups bread flour
- 1 cup one minute oatmeal
- 1 tsp salt
- 6 tsp white granulated sugar
- 1 Tbsp onion powder
- 1 Tbsp dried rosemary
- 1½ tsp bread machine yeast

Carbs – *27 g*   **Fat** – *3 g*   **Protein** – *5 g*   **Calories** – *123*

Directions

- Add each ingredient to the bread machine in the order and at the temperature recommended by your bread machine manufacturer.
- Close the lid, select the basic bread, medium crust setting on your bread machine and press start.

- *After the bread machine has finished kneading, sprinkle some rosemary on top of the bread dough.*
- *When the bread machine has finished baking, remove the bread and put it on a cooling rack.*

26 Chive Bread

Servings: 14 Slices   *Prep Time: 10 Min.*   *Cook Time: 3 H.*

Ingredients

- ⅔ cup milk (70°F to 80°F)
- ¼ cup water (70°F to 80°F)
- ¼ cup sour cream
- 2 Tbsp butter
- 1½ tsp sugar
- 1½ tsp salt
- 3 cups bread flour
- ⅛ tsp baking soda
- ¼ cup minced chives
- 2¼ tsp active dry yeast leaves

Carbs – 18 g   *Fat – 2 g*   *Protein – 4 g*   *Calories – 105*

Directions

- *Add each ingredient to the bread machine in the order and at the temperature recommended by your bread machine manufacturer.*
- *Close the lid, select the basic bread, medium crust setting on your bread machine and press start.*
- *When the bread machine has finished baking, remove the bread and put it on a cooling rack.*

27 Pumpkin Cinnamon Bread

Servings: *14 Slices*   **Prep Time:** *10 Min.*   **Cook Time:** *3 H.*

Ingredients

- *1 cup sugar*
- *cup canned pumpkin*
- *⅓ cup vegetable oil*
- *1 tsp vanilla*
- *2 eggs*
- *1½ cups all-purpose bread flour*
- *2 tsp baking powder*
- *¼ tsp salt*
- *1 tsp ground cinnamon*
- *¼ tsp ground nutmeg*
- *⅛ tsp ground cloves*

Carbs – 39 g   *Fat – 5 g*   *Protein – 3 g*   *Calories – 140*

Directions

- *Add each ingredient to the bread machine in the order and at the temperature recommended by your bread machine manufacturer.*
- *Close the lid, select the quick, medium crust setting on your bread machine and press start.*
- *When the bread machine has finished baking, remove the bread and put it on a cooling rack.*

28 Lavender Buttermilk Bread

Servings: **14 Slices**   Prep Time: **10 Min.**   Cook Time: **3 H.**

Ingredients

- ½ cup water
- ⅞cup buttermilk
- ¼ cup olive oil
- 3 Tbsp finely chopped fresh lavender leaves
- 1 ¼ tsp finely chopped fresh lavender flowers
- Grated zest of 1 lemon
- 4cups bread flour
- 2 tsp salt
- 2 ¾ tsp bread machine yeast

Carbs – **27 g**   Fat – **5 g**   Protein – **2 g**   Calories – **160**

Directions

- Add each ingredient to the bread machine in the order and at the temperature recommended by your bread machine manufacturer.
- Close the lid, select the basic bread, medium crust setting on your bread machine and press start.

- *When the bread machine has finished baking, remove the bread and put it on a cooling rack.*

29 Cajun Bread

Servings: *14 Slices* **Prep Time:** *10 Min.* **Cook Time:** *2 H.*

Ingredients

- *½ cup water*
- *¼ cup chopped onion*
- *¼ cup chopped green bell pepper*
- *2 tsp finely chopped garlic*
- *2 tsp soft butter*
- *2 cups bread flour*
- *1 Tbsp sugar*
- *1 tsp Cajun*
- *½ tsp salt*
- *1 tsp active dry yeast*

Carbs – 23 g *Fat – 4 g* *Protein – 5 g* *Calories – 150*

Directions

- *Add each ingredient to the bread machine in the order and at the temperature recommended by your bread machine manufacturer.*
- *Close the lid, select the basic bread, medium crust setting on your bread machine and press start.*
- *When the bread machine has finished baking, remove the bread and put it on a cooling rack.*

30 Turmeric Bread

Servings: *14 Slices*   **Prep Time:** *5 Min.*   **Cook Time:** *3 H.*

Ingredients

- 1 tsp dried yeast
- 4 cups strong white flour
- 1 tsp turmeric powder
- 2 tsp beetroot powder
- 2 Tbsp olive oil
- 1.5 tsp salt
- 1 tsp chili flakes 1⅜ water

Carbs – **24 g**   *Fat –* **3 g**   *Protein –* **2 g**   *Calories –* **129**

Directions

- Add each ingredient to the bread machine in the order and at the temperature recommended by your bread machine manufacturer.

- *Close the lid, select the basic bread, medium crust setting on your bread machine and press start.*
- *When the bread machine has finished baking, remove the bread and put it on a cooling rack.*

31 Rosemary Cranberry Pecan Bread

Servings: 14 Slices   *Prep Time: 30 Min.*   *Cook Time: 3 H.*

Ingredients

- *⅓ cups water, plus*
- *2 Tbsp water*
- *2 Tbsp butter*
- *2 tsp salt*
- *4 cups bread flour*
- *¾ cup dried sweetened cranberries*
- *¾ cup toasted chopped pecans*
- *2 Tbsp non-fat powdered milk*
- *¼ cup sugar*
- *2 tsp yeast*

Carbs – 18 g   *Fat – 5 g*   *Protein – 9 g*   *Calories – 160*

Directions

- *Add each ingredient to the bread machine in the order and at the temperature recommended by your bread machine manufacturer.*
- *Close the lid, select the basic bread, medium crust setting on your bread machine and press start.*
- *When the bread machine has finished baking, remove the bread and put it on a cooling rack.*

32 Sesame French Bread

Servings: *14 Slices*   **Prep Time:** *20 Min.*   **Cook Time:** *3 H.15 Min.*

Ingredients

- ⅞ cup water
- 1 Tbsp butter, softened
- 3 cups bread flour
- 2 tsp sugar
- 1 tsp salt
- 2 tsp yeast
- 2 Tbsp sesame seeds toasted

Carbs – 28 g   *Fat – 3 g*   *Protein – 6 g*   *Calories – 160*

Directions

- *Add each ingredient to the bread machine in the order and at the temperature recommended by your bread machine manufacturer.*
- *Close the lid, select the French bread, medium crust setting on your bread machine and press start.*
- *When the bread machine has finished baking, remove the bread and put it on a cooling rack.*

DID YOU KNOW?

12) Most of the bread marketed in the U.S. as "wheat" is actually white bread dyed brown with caramel food coloring.

13) Ben Hawkey, the actor in Game of Thrones who plays Hotpie, opened his own bakery and sells Direwolf shaped bread

14) Hawaiian sweet bread was brought to Hawaii by Portuguese immigrants

15) "Fairy Bread" is a common treat served at children's parties in Australia, consisting of buttered bread and sprinkles.

16) nearly 2,000-year-old loaf of bread was found during excavations in Herculaneum, and the recipe has been recreated by The British Museum.

VEGETABLE BREADS

33 Vegetable Bread

Servings: 14 Slices   *Prep Time: 15 Min.*   *Cook Time: 3 H.*

Carbs – 18 g   *Fat – 1 g*   **Protein – 4 g**   *Calories – 94*

Ingredients

- ½ cup warm buttermilk (70°F to 80°F)
- 3 Tbsp water (70°F to 80°F)
- 1 Tbsp canola oil
- ⅔ cup shredded zucchini
- ¼ cup chopped red sweet pepper

- *2 Tbsp chopped green onions*
- *2 Tbsp grated parmesan cheese*
- *2 Tbsp sugar*
- *1 tsp salt*
- *½ tsp lemon-pepper seasoning*
- *½ cup old-fashioned oats*
- *2½ cup bread flour*
- *1½ tsp active dry yeast Peppercorns*

Directions

- *Add each ingredient to the bread machine in the order and at the temperature recommended by your bread machine manufacturer.*
- *Close the lid, select the basic bread, medium crust setting on your bread machine and press start.*
- *When the bread machine has finished baking, remove the bread and put it on a cooling rack.*

34 Potato Bread

Servings: **14 Slices**   *Prep Time:* **5 Min.**   *Cook Time:* **3 H.10 Min.**

Ingredients

- ¾ cup milk
- ½ cup water
- 2 Tbsp canola oil
- 1½ tsp salt
- 3 cups bread flour
- ½ cup instant potato flakes
- 1 Tbsp sugar
- ¼ tsp white pepper
- 2 tsp active dry yeast

Carbs – 18 g   Fat – 2 g   Protein – 4 g   Calories – 90

Directions

- *Add each ingredient to the bread machine in the order and at the temperature recommended by your bread machine manufacturer.*
- *Close the lid, select the basic bread, medium crust setting on your bread machine, and press start.*
- *When the bread machine has finished baking, remove the bread and put it on a cooling rack.*

35 Carrot *Coriander Bread*

Servings: *14 Slices*   Prep Time: *15 Min.*   Cook Time: *3 H.*

Ingredients

- *2-3 freshly grated carrots,*
- *1⅛ cup lukewarm water*
- *2 Tbsp sunflower oil*
- *4 tsp freshly chopped coriander*
- *2½ cups unbleached white bread flour*
- *2 tsp ground coriander*
- *1 tsp salt*
- *5 tsp sugar*
- *4 tsp easy blend dried yeast*

Carbs – *12 g*   Fat – *5 g*   Protein – *2 g*   Calories – *98*

Directions

- *Add each ingredient to the bread machine in the order and at the temperature recommended by your bread machine manufacturer.*

- *Close the lid, select the basic bread, medium crust setting on your bread machine, and press start.*
- *When the bread machine has finished baking, remove the bread and put it on a cooling rack.*

36 Zucchini Bread

Servings: **7 Slices**   Prep Time: **10 Min.**   Cook Time: **40 Min.**

Ingredients

- ⅓ cup vegetable oil
- ¾ cup shredded zucchini
- 2 large eggs, room temperature
- ⅓ cup brown sugar, packed
- 3 Tbsp granulated sugar
- 1½ cups unbleached, all-purpose flour
- ¾ tsp ground cinnamon
- ¼ tsp ground allspice
- ¾ tsp salt
- ½ tsp baking soda
- ½ tsp baking powder
- ⅓ cup walnuts
- ⅓ cup raisins

Carbs – **5 g**   Fat – **3 g**   Protein – **2 g**   Calories – **126**

- *Add each ingredient to the bread machine in the order and at the temperature recommended by your bread machine manufacturer.*
- *Close the lid, select the cake/quick, medium crust setting on your bread machine and press start.*
- *When the bread machine has finished baking, remove the bread and put it on a cooling rack.*

37 Potato Dill Bread

Servings: *14 slices*   Prep Time: *15 min.*   Cook Time: *40min.*

Ingredients

- 1 (.25 oz) package active dry yeast
- ½ cup water
- 1 Tbsp sugar
- tsp salt
- 2Tbsp melted butter
- 1 package or bunch fresh dill
- ¾ cup room temperature mashed potatoes
- 2¼ cups bread flour

Carbs – *24 g*   Fat – *3 g*   Protein – *5 g*   Calories – *110*

Directions

- *Add each ingredient to the bread machine in the order and at the temperature recommended by your bread machine manufacturer.*
- *Close the lid, select the basic bread, medium crust setting on your bread machine, and press start.*
- *When the bread machine has finished baking, remove the bread and put it on a cooling rack.*

38 Sweet Potato Bread

Servings: **14 Slices**   Prep Time: **10 Min.**   Cook Time: **2 H.**

Ingredients

- ½ Cup Plus 2 Tbsp Water
- 1 Tsp Vanilla Extract
- 1 Cup Plain Mashed Sweet Potatoes
- 4 Cups Bread Flour
- ¼ Tsp Each Ground Nutmeg And Cinnamon
- 2 Tbsp Butter
- ⅓ Cup Dark Brown Sugar
- 1½ Tsp Salt
- 2 Tsp Active Dry Yeast
- 2 Tbsp Dry Milk Powder

Carbs – 21 G   Fat – 7 G   Protein – 1 G   Calories – 141

Directions

- *Add Each Ingredient To The Bread Machine In The Order And At The Temperature Recommended By Your Bread Machine Manufacturer.*
- *Close The Lid, Select The Basic Bread, Medium Crust Setting On Your Bread Machine, And Press Start.*
- *When The Bread Machine Has Finished Baking, Remove The Bread And Put It On A Cooling Rack.*

39 Cornmeal Bread

Servings: **14 Slices**   *Prep Time:* **10 Min.**   *Cook Time:* **2 H.10 Min.**

Ingredients

- *2½ tsp active dry yeast*
- *1 ⅓ cup water*
- *2 Tbsp dark or light brown sugar*
- *1 large beaten egg*
- *2 Tbsp softened butter*
- *1½ tsp salt*
- *¾ cup cornmeal*
- *¾ cup whole wheat flour*
- *2¾ cups white bread flour*

Carbs – 25 g   *Fat – 2 g*   *Protein – 4 g*   *Calories – 139*

Directions

- *Add each ingredient to the bread machine in the order and at the temperature recommended by your bread machine manufacturer.*
- *Close the lid, select the basic bread, medium crust setting on your bread machine, and press start.*
- *When the bread machine has finished baking, remove the bread and put it on a cooling rack.*

40 Basil Tomato Bread

Servings: *14 slices*   Prep Time: *10 min.*   Cook Time: *3 h.*

Ingredients

- *2¼ tsp dried active baking yeast*
- *1⅝ cups bread flour*
- *3 Tbsp wheat bran*
- *5 Tbsp quinoa*
- *3 Tbsp dried milk powder*
- *1 Tbsp dried basil*
- *25g sun-dried tomatoes, chopped*
- *1 tsp salt*
- *1⅛ cups water*
- *1 cup boiling water to cover tomatoes*

Carbs – *18 g*   Fat – *2 g*   Protein – *4 g*   Calories – *100*

Directions

- *Cover dried tomatoes with boiling water in a bowl.*
- *Soak for 10 minutes, drain, and cool to room temperature.*
- *Snip tomatoes into small pieces, using scissors.*
- *Add each ingredient to the bread machine in the order and at the temperature recommended by your bread machine manufacturer.*
- *Close the lid, select the basic bread, medium crust setting on your bread machine and press start.*
- *When the bread machine has finished baking, remove the bread and put it on a cooling rack.*

FRUIT BREADS

41 Fruit Raisin Bread

Servings: *14 slices*   **Prep Time:** *15 min.*   **Cook Time:** *3 h.5 min.*

Ingredients

- *1 egg*
- *1 cup water plus*
- *2 Tbsp*
- *½ tsp ground cardamom.*
- *1 tsp salt*
- *1½ Tbsp sugar*
- *¼ cup butter, softened*
- *3 cups bread flour*
- *1 tsp bread machine yeast*
- *⅓ cup raisins*
- *⅓ cup mixed candied fruit*

Carbs – *32 g*   **Fat** – *3 g*   **Protein** – *4 g*   **Calories** – *130*

Directions

- *Add each ingredient except the raisins and fruitcake mix to the bread machine in the order and at the temperature recommended by your bread machine manufacturer.*

- *Close the lid, select the basic bread, medium crust setting on your bread machine, and press start.*
- *Add raisins and fruit at the fruit/nut beep or 5 to 10 minutes before the last kneading cycle ends.*
- *When the bread machine has finished baking, remove the bread and put it on a cooling rack.*

42 Harvest Fruit Bread

Servings: **14 slices**   Prep Time: **10 min.**   Cook Time: **3 h.**

Ingredients

- 1 cup plus
- 2 Tbsp water (70°F to 80°F) 1 egg
- 3 Tbsp butter, softened
- ¼ cup packed brown sugar
- 1½ tsp salt
- ¼ tsp ground nutmeg Dash allspice
- 3¾ cups plus
- 1 Tbsp bread flour
- 2 tsp active dry yeast
- 1 cup dried fruit (dried cherries, cranberries and/or raisins)
- ⅓ cup chopped pecans

Carbs – 36 g   Fat – 6 g   Protein – 6 g   Calories – 214

Directions

- *Add each ingredient except the fruit and pecans to the bread machine in the order and at the temperature recommended by your bread machine manufacturer.*
- *Close the lid, select the basic bread, medium crust setting on your bread machine, and press start.*
- *Just before the final kneading, add the fruit and pecans.*
- *When the bread machine has finished baking, remove the bread and put it on a cooling rack.*

CHEESE BREAD

43 French Cheese Bread

Servings: *14 slices*   Prep Time: *5 min.*   Cook Time: *3 h.25 min.*

Ingredients

- *1 tsp sugar*
- *2¼ tsp yeast*
- *1¼ cup water*
- *3 cups bread flour*
- *2 Tbsp parmesan cheese*
- *1 tsp garlic powder*
- *1½ tsp salt*

Carbs – *21 g*   Fat – *6 g*   Protein – *8 g*   Calories – *170*

Directions

- *Add each ingredient to the bread machine in the order and at the temperature recommended by your bread machine manufacturer.*
- *Close the lid, select the basic bread, medium crust setting on your bread machine, and press start.*
- *When the bread machine has finished baking, remove the bread and put it on a cooling rack.*

44 Beer Cheese Bread

Ingredients

- 1 package active dry yeast
- 3 cups bread flour
- 1 Tbsp sugar
- 1½ tsp salt
- 1 Tbsp room temperature butter
- 1¼ cup room temperature beer
- ½ cup shredded or diced American cheese
- ½ cup shredded or diced Monterey jack cheese

Carbs – **21 g**   Fat – **5 g**   Protein – **5 g**   Calories – **144**

Directions

- Heat the beer and American cheese in the microwave together until just warm.
- Add each ingredient to the bread machine in the order and at the temperature recommended by your bread machine manufacturer.

- *Close the lid, select the basic bread, medium crust setting on your bread machine and press start.*
- *When the bread machine has finished baking, remove the bread and put it on a cooling rack.*

45 Jalapeno Cheese Bread

Servings: **14 slices**   Prep Time: **5 min.**   Cook Time: **3 h.**

Ingredients

- 3 cups bread flour
- 1½ tsp active dry yeast
- 1 cup water
- 2 Tbsp sugar
- 1 tsp salt
- ½ cup shredded cheddar cheese
- ¼ cup diced jalapeno peppers

Carbs – **22 g**   Fat – **4 g**   Protein – **7 g**   Calories – **150**

Directions

- Add each ingredient to the bread machine in the order and at the temperature recommended by your bread machine manufacturer.
- Close the lid, select the basic bread, medium crust setting on your bread machine, and press start.

- When the bread machine has finished baking, remove the bread and put it on a cooling rack.

46 Cheddar Cheese Bread

Servings: **14** Slices Prep Time: **5** Min. Cook Time: **3 H.10** Min.

Ingredients

- 1 cup lukewarm milk
- 3 cups all-purpose flour
- 1¼ tsp salt
- 1 tsp tabasco sauce, optional
- ¼ cup Vermont cheese powder
- 1 Tbsp sugar
- 1 cup grated cheddar cheese, firmly packed
- 1½ tsp instant yeast

Carbs – 24 g Fat – 5 g Protein – 7 g Calories – 165

Directions

- Add each ingredient to the bread machine in the order and at the temperature recommended by your bread machine manufacturer.
- Close the lid, select the basic bread, medium crust setting on your bread machine, and press start.
- When the bread machine has finished baking, remove the bread and put it on a cooling rack.

47 Cottage Cheese and Chive Bread

Servings: **14 Slices**   *Prep Time:* **10 Min.**   *Cook Time:* **3 H.**

Ingredients

- ⅜ cup water
- 1 cup cottage cheese 1 large egg
- 2Tbsp butter
- 1½ tsp salt
- 3¾ cups white bread flour
- 3 Tbsp dried chives
- 2½ Tbsp granulated sugar
- 2¼ tsp active dry yeast

Carbs – **33 g**   *Fat –* **5 g**   *Protein –* **7 g**   *Calories –* **196**

Directions

- *Add each ingredient to the bread machine in the order and at the temperature recommended by your bread machine manufacturer.*
- *Close the lid, select the basic bread, medium crust setting on your bread machine, and press start.*

- *When the bread machine has finished baking, remove the bread and put it on a cooling rack.*

48 Ricotta Bread

Servings: **14 Slices**   *Prep Time:* **5 Min.**   *Cook Time:* **3 H.15 Min.**

Ingredients

- *3 Tbsp skim milk*
- *⅔ cup ricotta cheese*
- *4 tsp unsalted butter, softened to room temperature*
- *1 large egg*
- *2Tbsp granulated sugar*
- *½ tsp salt*
- *1½ cups bread flour, + more flour, as needed*
- *1 tsp active dry yeast*

Carbs – 3 g   *Fat – 12 g*   *Protein – 11 g*   *Calories – 174*

Directions

- *Add each ingredient to the bread machine in the order and at the temperature recommended by your bread machine manufacturer.*
- *Close the lid, select the basic bread, medium crust setting on your bread machine, and press start.*

- *When the bread machine has finished baking, remove the bread and put it on a cooling rack.*

49 Oregano Cheese Bread

Servings: **14 slices**   Prep Time: **10 min.**   Cook Time: **2 h.5 min.**

Ingredients

- 3 cups bread flour 1 cup water
- ½ cup freshly grated parmesan cheese
- 3 Tbsp sugar
- 1 Tbsp dried leaf oregano
- 1½ Tbsp olive oil
- 1 tsp salt
- 2 tsp active dry yeast

Carbs – **22 g**   Fat – **5 g**   Protein – **3 g**   Calories – **146**

Directions

- *Add each ingredient to the bread machine in the order and at the temperature recommended by your bread machine manufacturer.*
- *Close the lid, select the basic bread, medium crust setting on your bread machine, and press start.*

- When the bread machine has finished baking, remove the bread and put it on a cooling rack.

50 Spinach and Feta Bread

Servings: 14 Slices   **Prep Time: 10 Min.**   **Cook Time: 4 H.15 Min.**

Ingredients

- 1 cup water
- 2 tsp butter
- 3 cups flour
- 1 tsp sugar
- 2 tsp instant minced onion
- 1 tsp salt
- 1¼ tsp instant yeast
- 1 cup crumbled feta
- 1 cup chopped fresh spinach leaves

Carbs – 16 g   *Fat – 6 g*   *Protein – 6 g*   *Calories – 140*

Directions

- *Add each ingredient except the cheese and spinach to the bread machine in the order and at the temperature recommended by your bread machine manufacturer.*
- *Close the lid, select the basic bread, medium crust setting on your bread machine, and press start.*
- *When only 10 minutes are left in the last kneading cycle add the spinach and cheese.*
- *When the bread machine has finished baking, remove the bread and put it on a cooling rack.*

51 Italian Cheese Bread

Servings: **14 slices** *Prep Time:* **10 min.** *Cook Time:* **3 h.**

Ingredients

- *1¼ cups water*
- *3 cups bread flour*
- *½ shredded pepper jack cheese*
- *2 tsp Italian seasoning*
- *2 Tbsp brown sugar*
- *1½ tsp salt*
- *2 tsp active dry yeast*

Carbs – 13 g *Fat – 6 g* *Protein – 7 g* *Calories – 130*

Directions

- *Add each ingredient to the bread machine in the order and at the temperature recommended by your bread machine manufacturer.*
- *Close the lid, select the basic bread, medium crust setting on your bread machine, and press start.*
- *When the bread machine has finished baking, remove the bread and put it on a cooling rack.*

DID YOU KNOW?

17) The first meal consumed on the moon was bread and wine. Buzz Aldrin brought with him communion bread and wine, along with a small silver chalice, and held communion during a requested radio blackout shortly after landing.

18) The soft inner part of bread is called the Crumb, not to be confused with crumbs

19) In Iceland, there's a traditional bread that you can bake in a pot by burying it in the ground near a hot spring

20) There was a project that challenged people to make an "Earth Sandwich" by placing pieces of bread in antipodal fashion on the earth (completely opposite of each other on the planet) For the first one, a baguette was placed in Spain and another in New Zealand.

21) Ciabatta is not a traditional Italian bread, it was invented in the 80s as a response to the popularity of baguettes.

22) A baker's dozen wasn't strictly 13. Baker's gave extra bread to avoid being penalized for selling short weight. So a dozen could be 13, 14 or even 15.

23) From 1266 until 2008 it was illegal in England to sell bread that weighed 600 grams

GRAIN, SEED AND NUT BREAD

52 Cranberry Walnut Bread

Servings: **14 Slices**	*Prep Time*: **10 Min.**	*Cook Time*: **3 H.**

Ingredients

- ¼ cup water
- 1 egg
- 3Tbsp honey
- 1½ tsp butter, softened
- 3¼ cups bread flour
- 1 cup milk
- 1 tsp salt
- ¼ tsp baking soda
- 1 tsp ground cinnamon
- 2½ tsp active dry yeast

- ¾ cup dried cranberries
- ½ cup chopped walnuts
- 1 Tbsp white vinegar
- ½ tsp sugar

Carbs – **24 g**	*Fat* – **2 g**	*Protein* – **4 g**	*Calories* – **130**

Directions

- *Add each ingredient except the berries and nuts to the bread machine in the order and at the temperature recommended by your bread machine manufacturer.*

94

- *Close the lid, select the basic bread, medium crust setting on your bread machine, and press start.*
- *Add the cranberries and walnuts around 5 minutes before the kneading cycle has finished*
- *When the bread machine has finished baking, remove the bread and put it on a cooling rack.*

53 Apple Walnut Bread

Servings: *14 slices*   **Prep Time:** *5 min.*   **Cook Time:** *2 h.30 min.*

Ingredients

- ¾ cup unsweetened applesauce
- 4 cups apple juice
- 1 tsp salt
- 3 Tbsp butter
- 1 large egg
- 4 cups bread flour
- ¼ cup brown sugar, packed
- 1¼ tsp cinnamon
- ½ tsp baking soda
- 2 tsp active dry yeast
- ½ cup chopped walnuts
- ½ cup chopped dried cranberries

Carbs – *15 g*   **Fat** – *8 g*   **Protein** – *3 g*   **Calories** – *130*

Directions

- *Add each ingredient to the bread machine in the order and at the temperature recommended by your bread machine manufacturer.*
- *Close the lid, select the basic bread, medium crust setting on your bread machine, and press start.*

- *When the bread machine has finished baking, remove the bread and put it on a cooling rack.*

54 Oat Nut Bread

Servings: **14 Slices**   Prep Time: **10 Min.**   Cook Time: **3 H.**

Ingredients

- *1¼ cups water*
- *½ cup quick oats*
- *¼ cup brown sugar, firmly packed*
- *1 Tbsp butter*
- *1½ tsp salt*
- *3cups bread flour*
- *¾ cup chopped walnuts*
- *1 package dry bread yeast*

Carbs – **22 g**   Fat – **3 g**   Protein – **4 g**   Calories – **120**

Directions

- *Add each ingredient to the bread machine in the order and at the temperature recommended by your bread machine manufacturer.*
- *Close the lid, select the rapid rise, medium crust setting on your bread machine, and press start.*

- When the bread machine has finished baking, remove the bread and put it on a cooling rack.

55 Pecan Raisin Bread

Servings: *14 Slices*   **Prep Time:** *10 Min.*   **Cook Time:** *3 H.*

Ingredients

- *1 cup plus*
- *2 Tbsp water (70°F to 80°F)*
- *8 tsp butter*
- *1 egg*
- *6 Tbsp sugar*
- *¼ cup nonfat dry milk powder*
- *1 tsp salt*
- *4 cups bread flour*
- *1 Tbsp active dry yeast*
- *1 cup finely chopped pecans*
- *1 cup raisins*

Carbs – 36 g   **Fat – 8 g**   **Protein – 6 g**   **Calories – 227**

Directions

- Add each ingredient to the bread machine except the pecans and raisins in the order and at the temperature recommended by your bread machine manufacturer.

- *Close the lid, select the basic bread, medium crust setting on your bread machine, and press start.*
- *Just before the final kneading, add the pecans and raisins.*
- *When the bread machine has finished baking, remove the bread and put it on a cooling rack.*

56 Soft Oat Bread

Servings: **14 Slices**   Prep Time: **15 Min.**   Cook Time: **3 H.**

Ingredients

- 1½ cups water (70°F to 80°F)
- ¼ cup canola oil
- 1 tsp lemon juice
- ¼ cup sugar
- 2 tsp salt
- 3 cups all-purpose flour
- 1½ cups quick-cooking oats
- 2½ tsp active dry yeast

Carbs – **21 g**   Fat – **3 g**   Protein – **3 g**   Calories – **127**

Directions

- *Add each ingredient to the bread machine in the order and at the temperature recommended by your bread machine manufacturer.*
- *Close the lid, select the basic bread, medium crust setting on your bread machine, and press start.*
- *When the bread machine has finished baking, remove the bread and put it on a cooling rack.*

57 Citrus and Walnut Bread

Servings: *14 Slices*   Prep Time: *10 Min.*   Cook Time: *3 H.*

Ingredients

- ¾ cup lemon yogurt
- ½ cup orange juice
- 5 tsp caster sugar
- 1 tsp salt
- 2.5 Tbsp butter
- 2 cups unbleached white bread flour
- 1½ tsp easy blend dried yeast
- ⅓ cup chopped walnuts
- 2 tsp grated lemon rind
- 2 tsp grated orange rind

Carbs – *23 g*   Fat – *6 g*   Protein – *7 g*   Calories – *160*

Directions

- *Add each ingredient except the walnuts and orange and lemon rind to the bread machine one by one, as per the manufacturer's instructions.*

- *Close the lid, select the basic bread, medium crust setting on your bread machine, and press start.*
- *Add the walnuts, and orange and lemon rind during the 2nd kneading cycle*
- *When the bread machine has finished baking, remove the bread and put it on a cooling rack.*

58 Quinoa Oatmeal Bread

Servings: **14 Slices**   *Prep Time:* **20 Min.**   *Cook Time:* **3 H.30 Min.**

Ingredients

- ⅓ cup uncooked quinoa
- ⅔ cup water (for cooking quinoa) 1 cup buttermilk
- 1 tsp salt
- 1 Tbsp sugar
- 1 Tbsp honey
- 4 Tbsp unsalted butter
- ½ cup quick-cooking oats
- ½ cup whole wheat flour
- 1½ cups bread flour

Carbs – **37 g**   *Fat –* **4 g**   *Protein –* **7 g**   *Calories –* **170**

Directions

- *Add quinoa to a saucepan. Cover it with water.*
- *Bring to boil. Cook for 5 minutes, covered.*
- *Turn off and leave the quinoa covered for 10 minutes.*
- *Add each ingredient to the bread machine in the order and at the temperature recommended by your bread machine manufacturer.*

- Close the lid, select the whole grain, medium crust setting on your bread machine and press start.
- When the bread machine has finished baking, remove the bread and put it on a cooling rack.

59 Multigrain Bread

Servings: *14 slices*   **Prep Time:** *5 min.*   **Cook Time:** *2-5 h.*

Ingredients

- 1⅛ cups water
- 3 Tbsp butter, at room temperature
- 1½ Tbsp honey
- ⅓ tsp salt
- ¾ cup 12-grain flour
- 2¼ cups whole wheat flour
- 1½ tsp bread machine yeast

Carbs – *21 g*   **Fat** – *3 g*   **Protein** – *4 g*   **Calories** – *117*

Directions

- Add each ingredient to the bread machine in the order and at the temperature recommended by your bread machine manufacturer.
- Close the lid, select the whole wheat, medium crust setting on your bread machine and press start.

- *3.When the bread machine has finished baking, remove the bread and put it on a cooling rack.*

60 Pesto Nut Bread

Servings: **14 slices**   Prep Time: **10 min.**   Cook Time: **3 h. 30 min.**

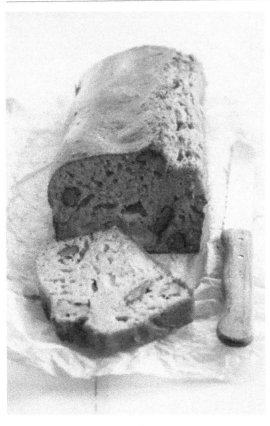

Ingredients

- *1 cup plus*
- *2 Tbsp water*
- *3 cups Gold Medal Better for Bread flour*
- *2 Tbsp sugar*
- *tsp salt*
- *1¼ tsp bread machine or quick active dry yeast*

For the pesto filling:

- *⅓ cup basil pesto*
- *2 Tbsp Gold Medal Better for Bread flour*
- *⅓ cup pine nuts*

Carbs – *31 g*   Fat – *6 g*   Protein – *5 g*   Calories – *190*

Directions

- *Add each ingredient to the bread machine in the order and at the temperature recommended by your bread machine manufacturer.*
- *Close the lid, select the basic bread, medium crust setting on your bread machine, and press start.*
- *In a small bowl, combine pesto and 2 Tbsp of flour until well blended. Stir in the pine nuts. Add the filling 5 minutes before the last kneading cycle ends.*
- *When the bread machine has finished baking, remove the bread and put it on a cooling rack.*

61 Seed Bread

Servings: **14 slices**	Prep Time: **5 min.**	Cook Time: **3 h. 5 min.**

Ingredients

- 3 Tbsp flax seed
- 1 Tbsp sesame seeds
- 1 Tbsp poppy seeds
- ¾ cup water
- 1 Tbsp honey
- 1 Tbsp canola oil
- ½ tsp salt
- 1½ cups bread flour
- 5 Tbsp wholemeal flour
- 1¼ tsp dried active baking yeast

Carbs – 19 g	Fat – 3 g	Protein – 4 g	Calories – 122

Directions

- Add each ingredient to the bread machine in the order and at the temperature recommended by your bread machine manufacturer.
- Close the lid, select the basic bread, medium crust setting on your bread machine, and press start.
- When the bread machine has finished baking, remove the bread and put it on a cooling rack.

62 Chia Seed Bread

Servings: **14 slices**   Prep Time: **10 min.**   Cook Time: **3 h. 30 min.**

Ingredients

- ¼ cup chia seeds
- ¾ cup hot water
- 2⅜ cups water
- ¼ cup oil
- ½ lemon, zest and juice
- 1¾ cups white flour
- 1¾ cups whole wheat flour
- 2 tsp baking powder
- 1 tsp salt
- 1 Tbsp sugar
- 2½ tsp quick rise yeast

Carbs – 28 g   Fat – 2 g   Protein – 6 g   Calories – 152

Directions

- Add the chia seeds to a bowl, cover with hot water, mix well and let them stand until they are soaked and gelatinous, and don't feel warm to touch
- Add each ingredient to the bread machine in the order and at the temperature recommended by your bread machine manufacturer.
- Close the lid, select the basic bread, medium crust setting on your bread machine, and press start.

- *When the mixing blade stops moving, open the machine and mix everything by hand with a spatula.*
- *When the bread machine has finished baking, remove the bread and put it on a cooling rack.*

MEAT BREADS

63 Garlic Pepperoni Bread

Servings: **14 slices**   *Prep Time:* **5 min.**   *Cook Time:* **3 h.**

Ingredients

- *1 cup water*
- *¼ cup light olive oil*
- *3 cups bread flour*
- *1 Tbsp sugar*
- *1 tsp salt*
- *½-1 tsp garlic powder*
- *½-1 Tbsp minced dried onions*
- *1 tsp dried basil*
- *¼ cup shredded mozzarella cheese*
- *⅓ cup grated parmesan cheese*
- *¼ cup pepperoni slice, chopped*
- *2 tsp bread machine yeast*

Carbs – 21 g   *Fat – 9 g*   *Protein – 14 g*   *Calories – 170*

Directions

- *Add each ingredient to the bread machine in the order and at the temperature recommended by your bread machine manufacturer.*

111

- *Close the lid, select the basic bread, medium crust setting on your bread machine, and press start.*
- *When the bread machine has finished baking, remove the bread and put it on a cooling rack.*

64 Meatloaf

Servings: 14 slices   **Prep Time:** 10 min.   **Cook Time:** 3 h. 20 min.

Ingredients

- *1 lb. ground pork 1 lb. ground turkey*
- *2 slices of soft bread, torn*
- *2 Tbsp minced onions*
- *2 eggs*
- *¾ cup milk*
- *½ tsp salt*
- *⅛ tsp black pepper*
- *⅛ tsp dry mustard*
- *⅛ tsp celery salt*
- *⅛ tsp garlic salt*
- *2 tsp Worcestershire sauce*

For the topping:

- *¾ cup ketchup*
- *3 Tbsp brown sugar*

Carbs – 20 g   Fat – 5 g   Protein – 24 g   Calories – 214

Directions

- *Add each ingredient except the toppings to the bread machine in the order and at the temperature recommended by your bread machine manufacturer.*
- *Close the lid, select the basic bread, medium crust setting on your bread machine and press start.*
- *Mix the topping ingredients (¾ cup ketchup with 3 Tbsp brown sugar) together.*
- *When the bread machine has finished baking, remove the bread and put it on a cooling rack.*
- *Cover the top of meatloaf with topping before serving.*

65 Sausage Herb and Onion Bread

Servings: **14 slices**   Prep Time: **10 min.**   Cook Time: **3 h.10 min.**

Ingredients

- ¾ tsp basil leaves
- 1½ Tbsp sugar
- ⅜ cup wheat bran
- 1 medium onion, minced
- 2¼ tsp yeast
- ¾ tsp rosemary leaves
- ½ Tbsp salt
- 1½ Tbsp parmesan, grated
- 3 cups bread flour
- ¾ tsp oregano leaves
- ¾ tsp thyme leaves
- 1⅛ cups water
- ¾ cup Italian sausage

Carbs – 34 g   Fat – 8 g   Protein – 15 g   Calories – 176

Directions

- Remove casing from sausage. Crumble the meat into a medium nonstick skillet.

114

- *Cook on medium heat, stirring and breaking up sausage until it begins to render its juices.*
- *Add onion and cook for 2-3 minuts until it softens and the sausage is no longer pink.*
- *Remove from heat and let it cool.*
- *Add each ingredient to the bread machine in the order and at the temperature recommended by your bread machine manufacturer.*
- *Close the lid, select the basic bread, medium crust setting on your bread machine, and press start.*
- *When the bread machine has finished baking, remove the bread and put it on a cooling rack.*

66 Cheddar and Bacon Bread

Servings: *14 slices*   **Prep Time:** *20 min.*   **Cook Time:** *2 h.20 min.*

Ingredients

- *⅓ cups water*
- *2 Tbsp vegetable oil*
- *1¼ tsp salt*
- *2 Tbsp plus*
- *1½ tsp sugar*
- *4 cups bread flour*
- *3 Tbsp nonfat dry milk*
- *2 tsp dry active yeast*
- *2 cups cheddar*
- *8 slices crumbled bacon*

Carbs *– 26 g*   **Fat** *– 5 g*   **Protein** *– 14 g*   **Calories** *– 171*

Directions

- *Add each ingredient to the bread machine except the cheese and bacon in the order and at the temperature recommended by your bread machine manufacturer.*

- *Close the lid, select the basic bread, medium crust setting on your bread machine, and press start.*
- *Add the cheddar cheese and bacon 30 to 40 minutes into the cycle.*
- *When the bread machine has finished baking, remove the bread and put it on a cooling rack.*

Did You Know?

24) Germany has the most diverse selection and production of bread in the world with 200 types of bread.

25) Bread become sweeter the longer you chew as your saliva starts to break down starch into sugars.

26) When the buttered bread is right side up and dropped from a table, there's an ~80% it will fall butter side down. This is because an average slice of buttered bread falling will complete a full turn in approx. 8 feet.

CHOCOLATE BREADS

67 Chocolate Cherry Bread

Servings: **14 slices**   *Prep Time:* **5 min.**   *Cook Time:* **3 h.**

Ingredients

- 1 cup milk
- 1 egg
- 3 Tbsp water
- 4 tsp butter
- ½ tsp almond extract
- 4 cups bread flour
- 3 Tbsp sugar
- 1 tsp salt
- 1¼ tsp active dry yeast
- ½ cup dried cherries, snipped
- ½ cup semisweet chocolate pieces, chilled

Carbs – **23 g**   *Fat* – **13 g**   *Protein* – **3 g**   *Calories* – **210**

Directions

- Add each ingredient to the bread machine in the order and at the temperature recommended by your bread machine manufacturer.
- Close the lid, select the sweet loaf, low crust setting on your bread machine, and press start.
- When the bread machine has finished baking, remove the bread and put it on a cooling rack.

68 Chocolate Orange Bread

Servings: *14 Slices*	Prep Time: *10 Min.*	Cook Time: *3 H. 10 Min.*

Ingredients

- *1⅝ Cups Strong White Bread Flour*
- *2 Tbsp Cocoa*
- *1 Tsp Ground Mixed Spice 1 Egg, Beaten*
- *½ Cup Water*
- *¼ Cup Orange Juice*
- *2 Tbsp Butter*
- *3 Tbsp Light Muscovado Sugar*
- *1 Tsp Salt*
- *1½ Tsp Easy Bake Yeast*
- *¾ Cup Mixed Peel*
- *¾ Cup Chocolate Chips*

Carbs – *35 g*	Fat – *6 g*	Protein – *2 g*	Calories – *197*

Directions

- *Sift The Flour, Cocoa, And Spices Together In A Bowl.*
- *Add Each Ingredient To The Bread Machine In The Order And At The Temperature Recommended By Your Bread Machine Manufacturer.*

121

- *Close The Lid, Select The Sweet Loaf, Medium Crust Setting On Your Bread Machine, And Press Start.*
- *Add The Mixed Peel And Chocolate Chips 5 To 10 Minutes Before The Last Kneading Cycle Ends.*
- *When The Bread Machine Has Finished Baking, Remove The Bread And Put It On A Cooling Rack.*

69 Almond Chocolate Chip Bread

Servings: *14 slices*   **Prep Time:** *10 min.*   **Cook Time:** *3 h.*

Ingredients

- *1 cup plus*
- *2 Tbsp water*
- *2 Tbsp softened butter*
- *½ tsp vanilla*
- *3 cups Gold Medal Better for Bread flour*
- *¾ cup semisweet chocolate chips*
- *3 Tbsp sugar*
- *1 Tbsp dry milk*
- *¾ tsp salt*
- *1½ tsp quick active dry yeast*
- *⅓ cup sliced almonds*

Carbs – *37 g*   **Fat –** *7 g*   **Protein –** *5 g*   **Calories –** *225*

Directions

- *Add each ingredient except the almonds to the bread machine in the order and at the temperature recommended by your bread machine manufacturer.*
- *Close the lid, select the sweet loaf, low crust setting on your bread machine, and press start.*

- Add almonds 10 minutes before last kneading cycle ends.
- When the bread machine has finished baking, remove the bread and put it on a cooling rack.

70 Walnut Cocoa Bread

Servings: **14 slices**   Prep Time: **10 min.**   Cook Time: **3 h.**

Ingredients

- ⅔ cup milk
- ⅓ cup water
- 5 Tbsp butter, softened
- ⅓ cup packed brown sugar
- 5 Tbsp baking cocoa
- 1 tsp salt
- 3 cups bread flour
- 2¼ tsp active dry yeast

- ⅔ cup chopped walnuts, toasted

Carbs – **23 g**   Fat – **7 g**   Protein – **5 g**   Calories – **168**

Directions

- Add each ingredient except the walnuts to the bread machine in the order and at the temperature recommended by your bread machine manufacturer.

- *Close the lid, select the sweet loaf, low crust setting on your bread machine, and press start.*
- *Just before the final kneading, add the walnuts.*
- *When the bread machine has finished baking, remove the bread and put it on a cooling rack.*

71 Mexican Chocolate Bread

*Servings: **14 slices***   *Prep Time: **10 min.***   *Cook Time: **3 h. 10 min.***

Ingredients

- *½ cup milk*
- *½ cup orange juice*
- *1 large egg plus 1 egg yolk*
- *3 Tbsp unsalted butter cut into pieces*
- *2½ cups bread flour*
- *¼ cup light brown sugar*
- *3 Tbsp unsweetened dutch-process cocoa powder*
- *1 Tbsp gluten*
- *1 tsp instant espresso powder*
- *¾ tsp ground cinnamon*
- *½ cup bittersweet chocolate chips*
- *2½ tsp bread machine yeast*

*Carbs – **32 g***   *Fat – **9 g***   *Protein – **5 g***   *Calories – **250***

Directions

- *Add each ingredient to the bread machine in the order and at the temperature recommended by your bread machine manufacturer.*
- *Close the lid, select the sweet loaf, low crust setting on your bread machine, and press start.*
- *When the bread machine has finished baking, remove the bread and put it on a cooling rack.*

72 Banana Chocolate Chip Bread

Servings: **14 slices**   Prep Time: **10 min.**   Cook Time: **2 h.**

Ingredients

- 2 eggs
- ⅓ cup melted butter
- ⅛ cup milk
- 2 mashed bananas
- 2 cups all-purpose bread flour
- ⅔ cup sugar
- 1¼ tsp baking powder
- ½ tsp baking soda
- ½ tsp salt
- ½ cup chopped walnuts
- ½ cup chocolate chips

Carbs – 36 g   Fat – 11 g   Protein – 4 g   Calories – 262

Directions

- *Add each ingredient to the bread machine in the order and at the temperature recommended by your bread machine manufacturer.*
- *Close the lid, select the quick bread, low crust setting on your bread machine, and press start.*
- *When the bread machine has finished baking, remove the bread and put it on a cooling rack.*

73 Chocolate Chip Bread

Servings: *14 Slices*   **Prep Time:** *5 Min.*   **Cook Time:** *3 H.*

Ingredients

- ¼ cup water
- 1 cup milk
- 1 egg
- 3 cups bread flour
- 3 Tbsp brown sugar
- 2 Tbsp white sugar
- 1 tsp salt
- 1 tsp ground cinnamon
- 1½ tsp active dry yeast
- 2 Tbsp margarine, softened
- ¾ cup semisweet chocolate chips

Carbs – 20 g   **Fat – 5 g**   **Protein – 5 g**   **Calories – 184**

Directions

- *Add each ingredient except the chocolate chips to the bread machine in the order and at the temperature recommended by your bread machine manufacturer.*
- *Close the lid, select the sweet loaf, low crust setting on your bread machine, and press start.*

- *Add the chocolate chips about 5 minutes before the kneading cycle has finished.*
- *When the bread machine has finished baking, remove the bread and put it on a cooling rack.*

COFFEE CAKES AND SWEET ROLLS

74 Chocolate Coffee Bread

*Servings: **14 Slices**   Prep Time: **10 Min.**   Cook Time: **3 H.***

Ingredients

- *1 ⅓ cups water*
- *⅓ cup cocoa powder*
- *1 ⅓ cups bread flour*
- *1 ⅓ cups whole wheat flour*
- *3 Tbsp powdered milk*
- *½ tsp salt*
- *1½ Tbsp honey*
- *2 envelopes instant mocha cappuccino mix*
- *2¼ tsp active dry yeast*
- *½ cup semi-sweet chocolate chips*

*Carbs – **23 g**   Fat – **9 g**   Protein – **12 g**   Calories – **210***

Directions

- *Add each ingredient except chips and mocha mix to the bread machine in the order and at the temperature recommended by your bread machine manufacturer.*
- *Close the lid, select the sweet loaf, low crust setting on your bread machine, and press start.*

- *Add the chocolate chips and mocha mix about 5 minutes before the kneading cycle has finished.*
- *When the bread machine has finished baking, remove the bread and put it on a cooling rack.*

75 Coffee Cake Banana Bread

Servings: 14 Slices   **Prep Time: 15 Min.**   **Cook Time: 3 H.**

Ingredients

- *4 medium bananas, mushed*
- *2 Tbsp brown sugar*
- *1½ tsp vanilla extract*
- *¾ tsp ground cinnamon*
- *½ cup butter, softened*
- *1 cup sugar*
- *2 eggs*
- *2 cups all-purpose flour*
- *1 tsp baking soda*
- *¼ tsp salt*
- *2 Tbsp Greek yogurt*

Carbs – 25 g   **Fat – 10 g**   **Protein – 4 g**   **Calories – 240**

Directions

- *Add each ingredient to the bread machine in the order and at the temperature recommended by your bread machine manufacturer.*

- *Close the lid, select the sweet loaf, low crust setting on your bread machine, and press start.*
- *When the bread machine has finished baking, remove the bread and put it on a cooling rack.*

76 Swedish Coffee Bread

Servings: 14 slices   *Prep Time: 10 min.*   *Cook Time: 2 h.40 min.*

Ingredients

- *cup milk*
- *½ tsp salt*
- *1 egg yolk*
- *2 Tbsp softened butter*
- *3 cups all-purpose flour*
- *⅓ cup sugar*
- *envelope active dry yeast*
- *3 tsp ground cardamom*
- *2egg whites, slightly beaten*

Carbs – 52 g   *Fat – 4 g*   *Protein – 7 g*   *Calories – 283*

Directions

- *Add each ingredient to the bread machine in the order and at the temperature recommended by your bread machine manufacturer.*

- *Select the dough cycle and press start.*
- *Grease your baking sheet.*
- *When the dough cycle has finished, divide the dough into three equal parts. Roll each part into a rope 12-14" long.*
- *Lay 3 ropes side by side, and then braid them together.*
- *Tuck the ends underneath and put onto the sheet. Next, cover the bread, using kitchen towel, and let it rise until it has doubled in size.*
- *Brush your bread with beaten egg white and sprinkle with pearl sugar.*
- *Bake until golden brown at 375°F in a preheated oven for 20-25 minutes.*
- *When baked, remove the bread and put it on a cooling rack.*

77 Cinnamon Rolls

Servings: 12 Rolls   Prep Time: 40 Min.   Cook Time: 2 H.

- *For the cinnamon roll dough:*
- *1 cup milk*
- *1 large egg*
- *4 Tbsp butter*
- *3 ⅓ cups bread flour*
- *3 Tbsp sugar*
- *½ tsp salt*
- *2 tsp active dry yeast*

For the filling:

- *¼ cup butter, melted*
- *¼ cup sugar*
- *2 tsp cinnamon*
- *½ tsp nutmeg*
- *⅓ cup nuts, chopped and toasted*

For the icing:

- *1 cup powdered sugar*
- *1 - 2 Tbsp milk*
- *½ tsp vanilla*

Carbs – 23 g   Fat – 5 g   Protein – 2 g   Calories – 140

Directions

- *Add each ingredient to the bread machine in the order and at the temperature recommended by your bread machine manufacturer.*
- *Select the dough cycle and press start.*
- *When it's done, transfer the dough onto a floured surface.*
- *Knead it for 1 minute, then let it rest for the next 15 minutes.*
- *Roll out a rectangle. Spread ¼ cup of melted butter over the dough.*
- *Sprinkle the dough with cinnamon, ¼ cup sugar, nutmeg, and nuts.*
- *Roll the dough, beginning from a long side. Seal the edges and form an evenly shaped roll. Cut it into 1-inch pieces.*
- *Put them on a greased baking pan.*
- *Cover with towel and leave for 45 minutes to rise.*
- *Bake at 375°F in a preheated oven for 20-25 minutes.*
- *Remove from the oven. Cool for 10 minutes.*
- *Mix the icing ingredients in a bowl. Adjust with sugar or milk to desired thickness.*
- *Cover the rolls with icing and serve.*

78 Texas Roadhouse Rolls

Servings: **18 Rolls**   *Prep Time:* **10 Min.**   *Cook Time:* **20min.**

Ingredients

- ¼ cup warm water (80°F - 90°F
- 1 cup warm milk (80°F - 90°F)
- 1 tsp salt
- 1½ Tbsp butter + more for brushing
- 1 egg
- ¼ cup sugar
- 3½ cups unbleached bread flour
- 1 envelope dry active yeast

For Texas roadhouse cinnamon butter:

- ½ cup sweet, creamy salted butter, softened
- ⅓ cup confectioners' sugar
- 1 tsp ground cinnamon

Carbs – 24 g   *Fat* – 1 g   *Protein* – 4 g   *Calories* – 170

Directions

- *Add each ingredient to the bread machine in the order and at the temperature recommended by your bread machine manufacturer.*
- *Select the dough cycle and press start.*
- *Once cycle is done, transfer your dough onto a lightly floured surface.*
- *Roll out the rectangle, fold it in half. Let it rest for 15 minutes.*
- *Cut the roll into 18 squares. Transfer them onto a baking sheet.*
- *Bake at 350°F in a preheated oven for 10-15 minutes.*
- *Remove dough from the oven and brush the top with butter.*
- *Beat the softened butter with a mixer to make it fluffy. Gradually add the sugar and cinnamon while blending. Mix well.*
- *Take out the rolls, let them cool for 2-3 minutes.*
- *Spread them with cinnamon butter on the top while they are warm.*

79 Orange Rolls

Servings: **20 Rolls**   Prep Time: **25 Min.**   Cook Time: **3 H.**

Ingredients

For the dough:

- ¼ cup heavy cream, warmed
- ½ cup orange juice concentrate
- 2 Tbsp sugar
- 1 tsp salt
- 1 large egg + 1 yolk
- 6 Tbsp unsalted butter, softened
- 3 cups all-purpose flour
- 2 tsp bread machine yeast

For the filling:

- 2 Tbsp unsalted butter, softened
- ½ cup sugar + 2 Tbsp grated orange zest mixture

For the icing:

- ¼ cup heavy cream
- ¼ cup sugar
- 2 Tbsp orange juice concentrate
- 2 Tbsp unsalted butter
- ⅛ tsp salt

Carbs – **26 g**   Fat – **9 g**   Protein – **3 g**   Calories – **19**

Directions

- *Add each ingredient for the dough to bread machine.*
- *Select the dough cycle and press start.*
- *When it is finished, the dough should have doubled in size*
- *Move the dough from the bread machine to a floured surface.*
- *Roll the dough into rectangle. Cover it with butter and the sugar- orange zest mixture.*
- *Roll the dough tightly from the long side. Cut into quarters. Then cut the quarters into 5 evenly-sized rolls.*
- *Put them onto greased pan, cover it with towel, and let them rise for 45 minutes in a warm place.*
- *Bake at 325°F in a preheated oven for 25-30 minutes.*
- *Add each of the icing ingredients to a saucepan. Mix and cook over a medium heat until the mixture is syrupy. Let it cool.*
- *Pour icing over warm rolls and serve.*

80 Apple Pecan Cinnamon Rolls

Servings: **12 rolls**   *Prep Time:* **30 min.**   *Cook Time:* **3 h.**

Ingredients

- *1 cup warm milk (70°F to 80°F)*
- *2 large eggs*
- *⅓ cup butter, melted*
- *½ cup sugar*
- *1 tsp salt*
- *4½ cups bread flour*
- *2½ tsp bread machine yeast*

For the filling:

- *3 Tbsp butter, melted*
- *1 cup finely chopped peeled apples*
- *¾ cup packed brown sugar*
- *⅓ cup chopped pecans*
- *2½ tsp ground cinnamon*

For the icing:

- *1½ cup confectioners sugar*
- *⅜ cup cream cheese, softened*
- *¼ cup butter, softened*
- *½ tsp vanilla extract*
- *⅛ tsp salt drained*

Directions

- *Add each ingredient for the dough to the bread machine in order stipulated by the manufacturer.*
- *Set to dough cycle and press start.*
- *When cycle has completed, place the dough onto a well-floured surface. Roll it into a rectangle. Brush it with butter.*
- *Mix the brown sugar, apples, pecans, and cinnamon in a bowl. Spread over the dough evenly.*
- *Beginning from the long side, roll the dough. Cut it into 1¾-inch slices.*
- *Transfer them onto a greased baking dish. Cover and let rise for 30 minutes.*
- *Bake at 325°F in a preheated oven for 25-30 minutes.*
- *Meanwhile, mix all the icing ingredients in a bowl.*
- *Take out the rolls and let them cool*
- *Cover warm rolls with the glaze and serve.*

HOLIDAY CAKES

81 Panettone

Servings: **14 slices**   Prep Time: **15 min.**   Cook Time: **3 h.10 min.**

Ingredients

- ¾ cup warm water
- 6 Tbsp vegetable oil
- 1½ tsp salt
- 4 Tbsp sugar
- 2 eggs
- 3 cups bread flour
- 1 (¼ ounce) package Fleishman's yeast
- ½ cup candied fruit
- ⅓ cup chopped almonds
- ½ tsp almond extract

Carbs – **21 g**   Fat – **6 g**   Protein – **4 g**   Calories – **198**

Directions

- Add each ingredient to the bread machine in the order and at the temperature recommended by your bread machine manufacturer.
- Close the lid, select the sweet loaf, low crust setting on your bread machine, and press start.
- When the bread machine has finished baking, remove the bread and put it on a cooling rack.

82 Julekake

Servings: *14 slices*   Prep Time: *30 min.*   Cook Time: *3 h.*

Ingredients

- ⅓ cup evaporated milk
- ⅔ cup water
- 1 egg, room temperature
- 3 ⅓ cups bread flour
- ¼ cup sugar
- ½ tsp salt
- ½ tsp cardamom
- ½ cup softened butter, cut up
- 2¼ tsp dry active yeast
- ½ cup golden raisins
- ⅔ cup candied fruit

Carbs – *57 g*   Fat – *3 g*   Protein – *8 g*   Calories – *297*

Directions

- Add each ingredient except the raisins to the bread machine in the order and at the temperature recommended by your bread machine manufacturer.
- Close the lid, select the basic bread, low crust setting on your bread machine, and press start.
- Add the raisins and fruit about 5 minutes before the kneading cycle has finished.

- *When the bread machine has finished baking, remove the bread and put it on a cooling rack.*

83 Christmas Bread

Servings: 8 slices   **Prep Time: 35 min.**   **Cook Time: 3 h.**

Ingredients

- *1¼ cups warm whole milk (70°F to 80°F)*
- *½ tsp lemon juice*
- *2 Tbsp butter, softened*
- *2 Tbsp sugar*
- *1½ tsp salt*
- *3 cups bread flour*
- *2 tsp active dry yeast*
- *¾ cup golden raisins*
- *¾ cup raisins*
- *½ cup dried currants*
- *1½ tsp grated lemon zest*

Glaze:

- *½ cup powdered sugar*
- *1½ tsp 2% milk*
- *1 tsp melted butter*
- *¼ tsp vanilla extract*

Carbs – 37 g   Fat – 2 g   Protein   Calories – 178

Directions

- *Add each ingredient except the raisins, currants, and lemon zest to the bread machine in the order and at the temperature recommended by your bread machine manufacturer.*
- *Close the lid, select the sweet loaf, low crust setting on your bread machine, and press start.*
- *Just before the final kneading, add the raisins, currants and lemon zest.*
- *When the bread machine has finished baking, remove the bread and put it on a cooling rack.*
- *Combine the glaze ingredients in a bowl.*
- *Drizzle over the cooled bread.*

84 Pumpernickel Bread

Servings: *14 slices*   **Prep Time**: *10 min.*   **Cook Time**: *3 h.*

Ingredients

- 1⅛ cups water
- ⅓ cup molasses
- ½ tsp lemon juice
- 1½ Tbsp canola oil
- 1½ cups bread flour
- 1 cup rye flour
- 1 cup whole wheat flour
- 1½ tsp salt
- 3 Tbsp cocoa powder
- 1½ Tbsp caraway seeds
- 2 tsp active dry yeast

Carbs – *19 g*   *Fat* – *1 g*   *Protein* – *3 g*   *Calories* – *97*

Directions

- *Add each ingredient to the bread machine in the order and at the temperature recommended by your bread machine manufacturer.*
- *Close the lid, select the wheat bread, dark crust setting on your bread machine, and press start.*
- *When the bread machine has finished baking, remove the bread and put it on a cooling rack.*

85 Italian Easter Cake

| Servings: **4 slices** | Prep Time: **10 min.** | Cook Time: **3 h.** |

Ingredients

- 1¾ cups wheat flour
- 2½ Tbsp quick-acting dry yeast
- 8 Tbsp sugar
- ½ tsp salt
- 3 chicken eggs
- ¾ cup milk
- 3 Tbsp butter
- 1 cup raisins

Carbs – **34 g** Fat – **5 g** Protein – **4 g** Calories – **190**

Directions

- Add each ingredient except the raisins to the bread machine in the order and at the temperature recommended by your bread machine manufacturer.
- Close the lid, select the sweet loaf, low crust setting on your bread machine, and press start.
- When the dough is kneading, add the raisins.
- When the bread machine has finished baking, remove the bread and put it on a cooling rack.

BREAD RECIPES FROM ALL OVER THE WORLD

150

86 Puerto Rican Pan Sobao

Prep: **45 mins**
Cook: **30 mins**
Rise: **90 mins**
Total: **2 h 45**
Servings: **24 servings**

Ingredients

- *1 1/2 cups/333 mL water (warm)*
- *4 1/2 teaspoons active dry yeast*
- *3 tablespoons white granulated sugar*
- *1/4 cup/51 grams lard (or shortening)*
- *5 cups/600 grams bread flour (divided)*
- *1 1/2 teaspoons salt*

Directions

- *Gather the ingredients. Divide up the bread flour: 3 cups (360 g) of flour in one bowl and the remaining 2 cups (240 g) in a separate one (you may not need all of it)*

- *Pour the warm water into a large mixing bowl. Stir in the yeast and sugar until completely dissolved. Let stand for 15 minutes so the yeast can bloom.*
- *Mix in the lard (or shortening). Use the paddle attachment if using a stand mixer, otherwise use a spoon or rubber spatula.*
- *Mix in the 3 cups of bread flour and salt. Add more bread flour in small amounts from the reserved bowl until the dough begins to follow the mixing spoon or paddle around the bowl.*
- *Switch to the mixer's dough attachment or, if kneading by hand, turn the dough out onto a lightly floured board. Knead for 10 minutes, adding a little more bread flour as needed. The dough should be elastic and smooth.*
- *Place the ball of dough in a greased bowl and flip it over so both sides are greased. Cover with a lint-free towel and let rise (also known as proofing) for 40 minutes, or until double in size.*
- *Punch down the dough.*
- *Turn out onto a very lightly floured board and fold four times. The only flour you should add from now on is just to prevent sticking.*
- *Form the dough into a ball, cover with a towel and let rest for 15 minutes.*
- *Divide the ball into two equal pieces. Form a ball with each, cover, and let them rest for 5 minutes.*
- *Using your palms, roll the dough back and forth to shape each ball into a 12-inch long baguette.*
- *Place the two loaves on a parchment-lined or lightly greased baking sheet. Cover and let rise for 30 minutes, until double in size.*
- *While proofing, preheat the oven to 400 F. Create a steamer by filling a deep pan with about 2 inches of water and place it on the top rack of the oven.*

- *Once risen, place the bread in the oven and bake for 25 to 30 minutes, until the top is golden brown and the bread sounds hollow when tapped.*
- *Let the bread cool for 5 minutes on the baking sheet, then transfer to a baking rack to cool completely (about 2 hours before slicing).*
- *Serve and enjoy*

87 Danish Kringle

Prep: 30 min

- *Cook: 20 min*
- *Rise Time: 2 h 30*
- *Total: 3 h 20*
- *Servings: 8 servings*

Ingredients

For the Dough:

- *2 cups bread flour (or all-purpose flour)*
- *4 tablespoons sugar*
- *2 teaspoons active dry yeast*
- *1 teaspoon ground cardamom*
- *6 tablespoons salted butter*
- *1 large egg*
- *5 tablespoons milk (warm)*

For the Filling:

- *6 tablespoons salted butter (softened)*
- *5 tablespoons pecans (chopped)*
- *5 tablespoons sugar*
- *2 teaspoons ground cinnamon*

For the Glaze:

- *1 egg (beaten)*
- *3 tablespoons sugar*

For the Icing:

- *3/4 cup confectioner's sugar*
- *3 to 4 teaspoons milk*

Directions

- *Gather the ingredients.*
- *For the dough, mix the flour, sugar, yeast, and cardamom in a large bowl.*
- *Make a well in the center. Melt the butter and while it is still warm (not hot) pour it into the center and add the egg.*
- *Mix with a wooden spoon, gradually adding the milk. (You may not need all of the milk. The dough should be soft, but not tacky.) Knead lightly.*
- *Place the dough in a lightly oiled bowl. Turn the dough in the bowl so the top is oiled. Cover with plastic wrap. Place in a warm place until doubled in size. This can take 2 to 3 hours, depending on the warmth of the kitchen.*

- *Meanwhile, make the filling. In a large bowl, mix together the softened butter, chopped pecans, sugar, and cinnamon. Line a baking sheet with parchment paper and grease the paper.*
- *On a large lightly floured surface, roll out the dough into a strip 5 inches wide and 32 inches long.*
- *Spread the prepared filling down the center.*
- *Flip over the two long sides of the dough, one on top of the other, pinching to enclose the filling.*
- *Transfer to the prepared baking sheet and form into a large oval, pinching the edges together to seal the oval. Cover lightly with a towel and allow to rise in a warm place for 30 minutes. Preheat the oven to 400 F.*
- *Just before baking, brush the dough with the beaten egg and sprinkle with sugar. Bake for 20 minutes, or until it turns a nice golden brown. Cool completely before frosting.*
- *Prepare the icing. In a large bowl, whisk together the confectioners' sugar and the milk, one teaspoon at a time, until desired spreadable consistency is achieved.*
- *Make the kringle icing*
- *Spread the icing over the top of the ring.*
- *Slice and serve.*

88 Pan de Jamón (Venezuelan Ham and Olive Bread)

Prep: 3 hrs *Cook: 35 mins* *Total: 3 hrs 35 mins* *Servings: 24 serving*

Ingredients

- *1/2 cup warm water*
- *1 tablespoon rapid rise yeast*
- *3 1/2 cups all-purpose flour*
- *1 stick butter (softened)*
- *2 tablespoons butter (melted)*
- *1 egg*
- 1/2 cup milk
- 3 tablespoons sugar
- 1/2 to 1 teaspoon salt
- 1/2-pound smoked ham (very thinly sliced)
- 1/2 cup raisins
- 1/2 cup sliced olives
- 1 egg yolk

Directions

- *Gather the ingredients*
- *Place the warm water in the bowl of a stand mixer.*
- *Sprinkle the yeast over the water and let stand for 5 minutes.*
- *Add 1 cup of the flour, the butter, and egg, and mix well using the dough hook attachment.*
- *Add the softened butter and another cup of flour and mix well.*
- *Add the remaining ingredients and knead until smooth, adding a bit of extra flour if the dough is too sticky. When well kneaded, the dough should be soft, shiny, and smooth.*
- *Place the dough in an oiled bowl. Cover with plastic wrap, set in a warm location, and let rise until doubled in bulk, about 30 minutes.*
- *Divide the dough in half. On a lightly floured surface, roll half of the dough into a large rectangle about 10 x 12 inches.*
- *Brush the dough with 1 tablespoon of the melted butter. Place half of the ham slices over the dough, leaving a 1-inch border all around.*
- *Sprinkle half of the raisins and half of the olives around over the ham.*
- *Tightly roll up the dough lengthwise starting with the long edge, sealing the last part of the dough to the roll with some water.*
- *Ham and olive on dough*
- *Place roll, seam side down, on a parchment-lined baking sheet, and tuck the ends under slightly. Repeat with the other half of dough.*
- *Roll dough*
- *Mix the egg yolk with a teaspoon of sugar and brush the mixture onto the rolls with a pastry brush.*

157

- *Lightly cover the rolls with oiled plastic wrap and let rise in a warm place for about an hour.*
- *Bake bread at 350 F for 30 to 40 minutes, until golden brown.*
- *Remove from oven, and let it cool slightly before slicing*

89 Tuscan Focaccia Bread

- *Prep: 20 min*
- *Cook: 35 min*
- *Proving Time: 2 h*
- *Total: 2 h55 mins*
- *Servings: 8 to 12*

Ingredients

- *2 3/4 cups bread flour*
- *1 teaspoon salt*
- *1 tablespoon instant yeast*
- *1/2 cup plus*
- *2 tablespoons extra-virgin olive oil (divided)*
- *1 cup warm water*
- *2 teaspoons sea salt flakes*

Directions

- *Gather the ingredients.*
- *Tuscan Focaccia Bread ingredients*

- *Place the flour, salt, yeast, 1 tablespoon of the olive oil, and the water into a stand mixer with a dough hook.*
- *place ingredients in stand mixer with dough hook*
- *Slowly mix the ingredients to form a sticky dough. Continue to mix for 4 to 5 minutes, adding more water if the dough feels dry.*
  focaccia dough in a stand mixer
- *Sprinkle the dough with 1 tablespoon of oil and mix for another few minutes to create a smooth, glossy dough.*
- *Dough in mixing bowl*
- *Cover and let rise in a warm, but not hot, place until doubled in size.*
- *dough doubles in size after rising*
- *Remove the dough from the bowl. Lay onto a baking sheet lined with parchment paper and lightly flatten into a rectangle, which is the traditional shape. You can also make your focaccia round if you wish. Leave to prove in a warm, but not hot, place for another hour.*
- *focaccia on a parchment lined baking sheet*
- *Preheat the oven to 425 F. Lightly press your fingertips into the dough, then drizzle with 1/2 cup olive oil, making sure the indentations are filled. Sprinkle all over with the sea salt.*
- *focaccia on baking sheet drizzled with oil*
- *Bake for 25 to 35 minutes. The bread is cooked when golden brown, risen, and hollow when gently tapped on the base.*
- *focaccia bread on a baking sheet*
- *Leave to cool on a rack.*
- *Serve and enjoy.*

90 German Seed Bread - Dreikernebrot

Ingredients

Dough 1:

- 1 1/4 cup/145 g. flour (whole wheat)
- 6 tbsp./50 g. flour (dark rye)
- 2 tsp. flaxseed (ground)
- 3/8 tsp. salt
- 5/8 cup water

Dough 2:

- *1 5/8 cup/193 g. flour (whole wheat)*
- *1/4 tsp. yeast (instant)*
- *1/2 cup water*

Finishing Dough:

- *6 tbsp./46 g. flour (whole-wheat)*
- *5 tbsp. sesame seeds*
- *5 tbsp. sunflower seeds (toasted)*
- *5 tbsp. pepitas (pumpkin seeds, toasted)*
- *1/2 tsp. salt*
- *2 tsp. yeast (instant)*
- *1 tbsp. honey*

Directions

- *Start the bread the evening before you want to bake it. Bring all ingredients to room temperature. In the first bowl mix the first 5 ingredients (Dough 1) until a soft ball forms.*
- *For the second bowl, mix the dry ingredients together with the flour until a dough ball can be formed. Knead for 2 minutes, let it rest and knead it again with wet hands. This "sponge" will rise slightly before morning. This dough should be tacky.*
- *Wrap dough 1 in plastic wrap and leave on your table overnight. Place dough 2 in an oiled bowl, cover with plastic wrap so it doesn't dry out, and refrigerate overnight.*

To Make the Finishing Dough

- *In the morning, remove dough 2 from the refrigerator at least an hour before you use it. Cut or pinch both doughs into several pieces and place together in a bowl.*
- *Sprinkle with the additional 6 tablespoons of flour. Add the sesame, sunflower, and pumpkin seeds, along with the salt, yeast (you may soften in 1 tablespoon water if it is not "instant" yeast) and honey and knead together for about 5 minutes.*
- *You should have a homogeneous dough by the end of this mixing (this may be done with a stand mixer and dough hook). If it is too sticky (not coming off your hands or spoon), you may add a small amount of flour, but since whole wheat flour soaks up a lot of water, try to add as little as possible.*

- *Turn out on a lightly floured board and knead for 3 minutes. Let rest 5 minutes. The dough should be firm but slightly tacky (sticks to hands slightly).*
- *After 5 minutes, knead again for 1 minute, form into a ball, place in a clean container and cover with a dish towel to let rise.*
- *Let rise at room temperature 1 to 2 hours, or until well risen (almost doubled). I keep my house at 58 F in the winter, so my rise took about 4 hours.*
- *For a free-standing hearth loaf, shape into a round shape or oval (do not knead again or you will remove air), draw the surface of the dough from top to bottom and pinch the dough closed on the bottom. Place on a greased cookie sheet. Decorate top if desired (wet with water to stick poppy seeds,*

162

sesame seeds or cracked wheat to loaf) and let rise until the loaf is not quite doubled in size. This will take 60 minutes to 2 hours.

- *About 20 minutes before you bake, start preheating your oven to 500 F. For free-standing loaf, place an old aluminum pan on the bottom rack and your baking rack on the next level up.*
- *Slash surface of bread with a sharp razor blade or very sharp knife to about 1/4 inch deep.*
- *To bake, place cookie sheet in the oven, pull bottom rack with old pan out and pour about 2 cups of water into it. Close quickly. If you have a spray bottle with water, open oven after 3 and 6 minutes and give 10 quick squirts onto the walls of the oven. Turn oven down to 450 F after 10 minutes and bake for 30 to 40 more minutes, or until the internal temperature of the bread reaches 200 F.*
- *Allow loaf to cool completely before slicing or it will still be wet on the inside.*

91 Italian Ciabatta Bread

- Prep: *15 mins*
- Cook: *25 mins*
- Prove *Time: 2 hrs*
- Total: *2 hrs 40 mins*

Ingredients

- 5 cups white bread flour (sifted)
- 2 teaspoons kosher salt
- 1 tablespoon dried yeast
- 3 tablespoons extra virgin olive oil
- 1 1/2 cups water (warm, but not hot)

Directions

- Gather the ingredients and line two baking sheets with parchment paper.
- Place the flour and salt into the bowl of a stand mixer and stir lightly to combine before sprinkling in the yeast.

164

- *Add all the oil and 1 cup of the water, reserving the rest to use as needed, then start to mix on a slow speed initially to bring the dough together. If you start too fast, the flour will fly everywhere.*
- *Increase the speed gradually. As the dough starts to form, add in the remaining water a little at a time until you have a dough sticky enough to cling to the side of the bowl. At this point, increase the speed to bring the dough together and start kneading. A dough hook will variously throw the dough around the bowl and pull it back together thus creating a silky smooth and well-kneaded dough in about 8 minutes.*
- *Oil a bowl large enough to hold roughly three times the dough you have in the mixer. Hold the mixer bowl over it and let the dough slowly slide inside. Do not be tempted to prod or poke the dough, simply cover with a tea cloth and put into a warm, but not hot, draft-free place and leave it to do its thing and prove for 2 hours or until the dough had tripled in size.*
- *Once the dough is ready, preheat the oven to 425 F.*
- *Heavily dust your work surface with flour. Remove the cloth, then let the dough slip from the bowl and take care not to be too heavy with it. It is incredibly light and should full of bubbles, which you want to keep. Slowly and carefully stretch the dough into a square approximately 12 inches x 12 inches, but don't be too precious about the size; you should not pull it so much that it tears.*
- *Generously sprinkle the surface of the bread dough with flour. Cut the dough evenly to create three rectangles 12 inches x 4 inches. Dust your hands with flour and lift the loaves one by one onto the baking sheet, stretching again just a little. You may find that where you have handled the ends of the loaves will widen slightly. This is the traditional shape of ciabatta and what gives it its name, which translates to "slipper" in English.*

- *Let the dough rest covered under a cloth for 15 minutes, then bake for 20 to 25 minutes in the oven. The ciabatta is cooked once it sounds hollow when tapped on the bottom. If you can resist not eating it, leave to cool on a rack, but don't leave it too long before as it genuinely is at its best when just a tad warm.*
- *Enjoy!*

92 Russian Sourdough Dark Rye Bread

- Prep: 30 mins
- Cook: 45 mins
- Total: 75 mins
- Servings: 20 servings

Ingredients

Rye Sour:

- *1 package/2 1/4 teaspoons yeast (instant, not rapid rise yeast)*
- *1 cup water (warm to the wrist)*
- *1 1/2 cups flour (medium rye)*

- *1 slice onion (raw, thick)*

Dough:

- *1/4 cup water (warm to the wrist)*
- *1 package / 2 1/4 teaspoons yeast (instant, not rapid rise yeast)*
- *1/2 teaspoon sugar*
- *4 1/2 cups flour (unbleached, all-purpose)*
- *1 cup water (boiling)*
- *1/2 cup pumpernickel or coarse rye meal*
- *1/4 cup cooking oil*
- *1 1/2 teaspoons salt*
- *1/4 cup molasses*
- *4 1/2 teaspoons coffee (instant)*
- *1/2-ounce chocolate (unsweetened)*
- *2 cups flour (medium rye)*

Directions

- *Rye Sour: Dissolve yeast in 1/2 cup water and blend in 3/4 cup rye flour. Stir in onion, cover with plastic wrap and set aside at room temperature. Let the sour rise and fall back. After this, stir the sour twice a day for three days. Remove onion and add remaining 1/2 cup water and remaining 3/4 cup rye flour. Cover and set aside. When the sour has risen and fallen once more (probably 1 more day), it is ready to use.*
- *Activate the Yeast: In a small bowl, combine 1/4 cup warm water, yeast, sugar and 1/4 cup of the all-purpose flour. Cover and set aside for 15 minutes or until bubbly.*

- *Make the Dough: Meanwhile, in a large bowl or the bowl of a stand mixer, combine the boiling water, pumpernickel, oil, salt, molasses, instant coffee, and chocolate. When this has cooled, add the rye sour, yeast mixture, 2 cups medium rye flour and the remaining 4 1/4 cups all-purpose flour. Mix until dough comes away from the sides of the bowl, then knead 5 minutes.*
- *Let the dough rest, covered, for 5 minutes and then knead another 5 minutes. Lightly coat a large bowl with cooking spray and place the dough in it, turning once to oil the top. Cover and let rise until doubled.*
- *Punch down dough and divide in half. Shape each into a round or oblong loaf and place on a parchment-lined baking sheet sprinkled with cornmeal. Cover and let rise until doubled.*
- *About 15 minutes before you want to bake, place a pan on the lowest rack of the oven for water to be added to create steam, and place another oven rack directly above it for the bread. Heat oven to 375 degrees.*
- *When ready to bake, slash the loaves with a lame bread-slashing tool or razor blade up to three times diagonally or once lengthwise and brush them with cold beaten egg whites.*
- *Pour 2 or 3 cups of water into the pan to create steam. Place loaves on the rack directly above. Bake 35-40 minutes or until an instant-read thermometer registers 195-200 degrees. Remove from oven and turn out of pans. Let cool completely on a wire rack. Rye bread has a gummy texture if eaten hot.*

93 Swedish Sweet Yeasted Bread (Vetebröd)

- **Prep**: 2 hrs 30 mins
- **Cook**: 25 mins
- **Total**: 2 hrs 55 mins
- **Servings**: 16 servings

Ingredients

- 2 1/2 cups milk
- 1 1/2 cups butter (melted)
- 1 cup sugar
- 1 tsp. salt
- 2 tsp. cardamom (freshly ground from about 25 cardamom pods)
- 4 1/2 tsp. dry active yeast
- 9 cups flour (all-purpose or bread flour)
- 1 egg (plus 2 tbsp. water, lightly beaten together into an egg wash)
- Pearl sugar (or crushed sugar cubes)

- *Chopped or slivered almonds*

Directions

- *Prepare your basic cardamom bread dough using the first 7 ingredients listed above (this takes about 1 1/2 hours).*
- *After punching down dough following its first rise, remove from bowl and knead lightly on a floured counter until smooth and shiny. Divide dough into two halves.*
- *Divide each half of the dough into three equal portions. Roll each portion into a long, thin "snake" (about 18 inches long). Braid three of the "snakes" together, folding and pinching outer edges under to form a loaf shape. Repeat for the second set of three dough "snakes." (Alternative: Do not divide dough into 2 halves, but separate entire mass into three equal portions. Roll the three portions into "snakes," braid together, then join and pinch ends together to form a single braided bread wreath).*
- *Place the two braided loaves (or the single braided wreath) on a greased baking sheet, cover with a towel, and let rise until doubled, about 45 minutes. Preheat oven to 375 F.*
- *When loaves (or wreath) have doubled, brush with egg wash and sprinkle with pearl sugar and/or almonds. Place in the middle of a preheated oven and bake for 25 minutes, or until done.*

94 Moroccan White Bread (Khobz)

- Prep: **20 mins**
- Cook: *20 mins*
- Rising times: **75 mins**
- Total: **115 mins**
- Servings: **8 servings**

Ingredients

- 4 cups flour (high-gluten or bread flour preferred)
- 2 teaspoons salt
- 2 teaspoons sugar
- 1 tablespoon yeast (active dry)
- 2 tablespoons vegetable oil
- 1 1/4 cups warm water

Directions

- Gather the ingredients.

171

- *Ingredients for Moroccan white bread*
- *Prepare two baking sheets by lightly oiling them or by dusting the pans with a little cornmeal or semolina.*
- *Prepare baking sheets*
- *Mix the flour, salt, and sugar in a large bowl. Make a large well in the center of the flour mixture and add the yeast.*
- *Mix flour, salt and sugar*
- *Add the oil and the water to the well, stirring with your fingers to dissolve the yeast first, and then stirring the entire contents of the bowl to incorporate the water into the flour.*
- *Add oil and water*
- *Turn the dough out onto a floured surface and begin kneading the dough, or use a stand mixer fitted with a dough hook. If necessary, add flour or water in very small amounts to make the dough soft and pliable, but not sticky. Continue kneading for 10 minutes by hand (or 5 minutes by machine), or until the dough is very smooth and elastic.*
- *Turn dough*
- *Divide the dough in half and shape each portion into a smooth circular mound. (If you prefer, you can divide the dough into four to six smaller loaves instead.) Place the dough onto the prepared pans, cover with a towel and allow it to rest for 10 to 15 minutes.*
- *Divide dough*
- *After the dough has rested, use the palm of your hand to flatten the dough into circles about 1/4-inch thick. Cover with a towel and let rise about 1 hour (longer in a cold room), or until the dough springs back when pressed lightly with a finger.*

172

- *Flatten dough*
- *Pre-heat oven to 435 F/225 C.*
- *Create steam vents by scoring the top of the bread with a very sharp knife or by poking the dough with a fork in several places.*
- *Bake the bread for about 20 minutes—rotating the pans about halfway through the baking pans—or until the loaves are nicely colored and sound hollow when tapped. Transfer the bread to a rack or towel-lined basket to cool.*

95 Naan (Leavened Indian Flatbread)

- *Prep:* **25 mins**
- *Cook:* **18 mins**
- *Rising/Proofing Time*: **100 mins**
- *Total:* **2 hrs 23 mins**
- *Servings:* **8 servings**
- *Yields:* **8 pieces**

Ingredients

- 1 1/2 teaspoons dry yeast
- 1 1/2 teaspoons sugar
- 1 cup/8 ounces warm water
- 3 cups/13 1/2 ounces all-purpose flour
- 1 teaspoon salt
- 6 tablespoons ghee, divided
- 3 tablespoons unsweetened yogurt
- Vegetable oil, for greasing
- 3 teaspoons onion seeds (aka nigella seeds or kalonji)

Directions

- *Gather the ingredients.*
- *Add the dry yeast and sugar to the warm water and stir till the yeast is dissolved. Cover and leave aside for 10 minutes or until the mixture begins to froth. This indicates the yeast is active. Keep aside.*
- *Mix the flour and salt to taste and sift through a very fine sieve into a large mixing bowl.*
- *Next, add the yeast mixture, 3 tablespoons of ghee, and all the yogurt. Use your fingertips to mix all this into a soft dough.*
- *Once mixed, flour a clean, flat surface, and knead the dough till it is smooth and stretchy.*
- *Grease a large bowl with a few drops of vegetable oil and put the dough in it. Cover with cling wrap and allow to rest for about 90 minutes or till the dough doubles in volume.*
- *Punch the dough down and knead again for 10 minutes.*
- *Equally, divide the dough and roll between your palms to form 8 round balls.*
- *Lightly flour the same surface on which you kneaded the dough and roll out each ball until you have a circle, 7 to 8 inches in diameter (1/4-inch thick). Gently pull on one edge of the circle to form the naan into a teardrop shape. Do not pull too hard or you may tear the dough. Instead of rolling the dough out (with a rolling pin) you can also pat it into a circle with your hands.*
- *Preheat oven 400 F / 200 C / Mark 6. Lay a piece of aluminum foil on an oven tray (to cover) and grease it lightly with a few drops of vegetable oil.*
- *Place as many formed dough balls as will fit without touching each other on the tray.*

- *Brush each dough ball lightly with ghee, and sprinkle a pinch of onion seeds evenly over the surface.*
- *Place the tray in the oven and cook till the naan begins to puff out and lightly brown. Flip the naan and repeat.*
- *Remove from oven and serve hot in a foil-lined basket.*

96 Classic and Crusty French Bread

- Prep:**20 mins**
- Cook:**30 mins**
- Rise Time:**105 mins**
- Total:2 hrs 35 mins
- Servings:**20 servings**
- Yields: **2 loaves**

Ingredients

- 2 cups warm water (95 F to 110 F)
- 2 1/4 teaspoons active dry yeast
- 2 tablespoons sugar
- 2 teaspoons salt
- 5 1/2 cups bread flour (approximately)
- Optional: 1 large egg white (lightly beaten)
- Optional: sesame seeds or poppy seeds

Directions

- Gather the ingredients.
- In a large bowl, combine water, yeast, sugar, and salt. Stir until dissolved.
- Mix in flour, a little at a time, until a soft dough is formed.

- *Turn dough out onto a floured board and knead it for about 8 minutes.*
- *Put the dough in a greased bowl and flip the dough over so that all of the dough including the dough top is lightly greased. Cover with a clean kitchen towel and let rise in a warm, draft-free place for about 1 hour or until double in size.*
- *Punch down the dough.*
- *Give the dough a quick 2-minute knead.*
- *Divide the dough into 2 equal halves. Shape each half into a long loaf.*
- *Place loaves onto a lightly greased baking sheet. Make about 5 diagonal slits, 3/4-inch deep, into the top of each loaf.*
- *Cover loaves and let rise for 45 minutes or until double in size.*

- *While the dough is proofing again, heat the oven to 400 F.*
- *Optional: Brush the loaves with beaten egg white for a shiny crust, and sprinkle with sesame or poppy seeds.*
- *Bake at 400 F for 5 minutes.*
- *Remove loaves from oven and use a mister to lightly spray the tops of loaves with cold water.*
- *Turn oven down to 350 F and bake loaves for another 25 minutes or until done.*
- *Remove loaves from baking sheet and let cool on a rack.*

97 Mexican Day of the Dead Bread (Pan de Muerto)

- Prep: **3 hrs**
- Cook: **40 mins**
- Total: **3 hrs 40 mins**
- Servings: **8 servings**

Ingredients

- 4 ounces butter (at room temperature)
- 3/4 cup white sugar
- 3 teaspoons whole aniseed
- 1 teaspoon salt
- 6 cups flour (white bread or all-purpose, divided)
- 4 large eggs (at room temperature)
- 1 1/4 cups warm water (not to exceed 110 F)
- 2 tablespoons orange zest
- 2 (1/4-ounce) packets instant dry yeas

Directions

- *Gather the ingredients.*
- *In the bowl of a stand mixer, combine butter, sugar, aniseed, salt, and 1/2 cup of the flour.*
- *Use the dough hook to mix the ingredients until they begin to come together.*
- *In a separate small bowl, whisk together the eggs, water, and orange zest.*
- *Add this to the stand mixer bowl, along with another 1/2 cup of the flour. Mix until combined.*
- *Add the yeast and another 1/2 cup of flour, mixing to combine.*
- *Add the remaining flour 1 cup at a time, mixing between additions, until a dough forms.*
- *Turn the dough out onto a floured surface and knead it for 1 minute.*
- *Cover it with a clean, damp dishcloth and let rise in a warm area for 1 hour and 30 minutes.*
- *Separate about 1/4 of the dough and use it to make bone shapes to drape across the loaf.*
- *Shape the rest of the dough into a flat-bottomed semi-sphere. Position the bone shapes on the top of the loaf and press gently so they adhere. Let the dough rise for an additional hour.*
- *Bake the loaf in a 350 F oven for about 40 minutes (30 minutes for smaller loaves).*
- *Cool and glaze, if desired, before serving.*
- *Cut pan de muerto into large wedges for eating by hand. Serve it with Mexican hot chocolate or champurrado (chocolate atole) if you like.*

98 Irish Soda Bread

- *Prep:* **15 mins**
- *Cook:* **45 mins**
- *Total:* **60 mins**
- *Servings:* **6**
servings

Ingredients

- *1 1/2 cups all-purpose flour*
- *1 cup whole wheat flour*
- *1 teaspoon baking soda*
- *1/2 teaspoon salt*
- *1/4 cup dried currants*
- *1 1/4 to 1 1/2 cups buttermilk*
- *1 tablespoon butter, melted, plus more for serving*

Directions

- *Gather the ingredients.*
- *Cover a large baking sheet with parchment paper. Preheat the oven to 425 F.*
- *In a large bowl combine the all-purpose flour, whole wheat flour, baking soda, and salt.*
- *Stir in the dried currants.*
- *Add 1 1/4 cups of buttermilk and stir until the dry ingredients are moistened. (Add more buttermilk, if necessary, to make a soft dough.)*
- *Turn the dough onto a lightly floured surface.*
- *Knead gently for about one minute to incorporate the ingredients and begin to shape the loaf.*
- *Shape into a ball and place on prepared baking sheet. Pat into an 8-inch circle.*
- *Using a sharp knife or razor blade, cut a 1/2-inch deep X in the top of the dough. Bake for about 45 minutes or until golden.*
- *Transfer to a wire rack, and brush with melted butter.*
- *Serve hot or at room temperature.*

99 Pan de Agua: Puerto Rican Water Bread

- *Prep:* **2 hrs 30 mins**
- *Cook:* **35 mins**
- *Total:* **3 hrs 5 mins**
- *Servings:* **8 to 10 servings**
- *Yields:* 2 loaves

Ingredients

- 1 packet dry active yeast
- 1 tablespoon sugar
- 2 cups water (warm)
- 1 tablespoon salt
- 5 cups all purpose flour
- 2 tablespoons cornmeal or flour (for dusting the baking board)
- 2 large egg whites
- 2 tablespoons water
- 1 cup water(boiling)

Directions

- Mix together the yeast, sugar, and 2 cups warm water in a large mixing bowl. Cover the mixture and let it stand for about 20 minutes until the yeast forms a foam on the top.

- *In a separate mixing bowl, mix together the salt and flour.*
- *Add the flour mixture to the yeast mixture 1 cup at a time. The dough will begin to form as you add the flour.*
- *Knead the dough for 10 to 15 minutes after you've added the last of the flour. It should become elastic and no longer sticky.*
- *Grease a large bowl and place the ball of kneaded dough inside. Cover the bowl and let the dough rise for 1 1/2 to 2 hours. The dough should double in size.*
- *Flour a work area and place the risen dough on it. Separate the dough into 2 equal portions and knead them into separate long loaves, about 12 to 14 inches.*
- *Sprinkle some cornmeal or flour on a baking board or cookie sheet large enough to hold both loaves. Place the loaves on the board or sheet and make 3 to 4 slashes along the top of each with a sharp knife.*
- *Mix together the egg whites and the 2 tablespoons water. Brush the egg mixture on top of the loaves.*
- *Place the loaves on the center rack of a cold oven, then place a shallow baking pan on the rack below the loaves. Fill the shallow pan with 1 cup boiling water.*

- *Wait 10 minutes, then turn the oven to 400 F. Bake the loaves for 35 minutes. Their internal temperature should reach 200 F and they should be golden and a little crusty. Serve warm.*

100 Danish Rye Bread

•*Prep:* 3 hrs
•*Cook:* 90 mins
•*Total:* 4 hrs 30 mins

Ingredients

- *80g buttermilk*
- *60g dark beer*
- *10g honey*
- *170g whole spelt flour*
- *65g dark rye flour*
- *90g whole flax seeds*
- *45g hulled hemp seed*
- *45g sunflower seeds*
- *14g salt*
- *230g whole rye berries*

- *220g water*
- *150g active sourdough starter*

Directions

- *Fully submerge the rye berries in water and soak them for twelve hours. Drain them after soaking.*
- *Add all ingredients to a large bowl and mix until well combined.*
- *Cover the bowl and leave it somewhere around 70 to 75 F to ferment for about 3 hours. After that time you should notice some visible fermentation activity. Due to the quality of the gluten, as well as all the heavy whole grains and seeds, the dough won't rise much, but if you don't see any bubbles, etc. then keep waiting, up to a maximum of 5 hours.*
- *Butter or oil a 4x9 Pullman-style loaf pan with a sliding lid, and using a flexible dough scraper, gently pour the dough into the open pan. It should fill about half the space.*
- *Let the dough ferment (technically, "proof" - the term for fermentation that takes place after the loaf has been shaped) for 2 more hours at the same ambient temperature.*
- *Refrigerate the dough in the covered pan for 12 to 16 hours.*
- *Preheat the oven to 425 F. Remove the pan, cover on, from the refrigerator and put it into the hot oven. After 20 minutes, remove the pan's cover and continue to bake for another 55-70 minutes, or until a thermometer inserted in the center of the loaf reads at least 205 F.*
- *Remove the loaf to a cooling rack. After the loaf has cooled to room temperature, wrap it in a clean kitchen towel. Wait 24 hours before slicing.*

101 Slovenian Potato Bread Recipe - Krompirjev Kruh

- Prep: **30 mins**
- Cook: **40 mins**
- Rise Time: **2 h**
- Total: **3 h 10 mins**
- Servings: **24 servings**

Ingredients

- 1 1/2 cups water
- 1 medium potato (peeled and cubed)
- 1 cup buttermilk
- 3 tablespoons sugar
- 2 tablespoons butter
- 2 teaspoons salt
- 6 to 6 1/2 cups good-quality all-purpose flour

- *2 (1/4-ounce) packages active dry yeast*

Directions

- *In a saucepan, cook potato, covered, in 1 1/2 cups water about 12 minutes or until tender. Do not drain. Mash potato in the water. Measure the potato-water mixture. If necessary, add additional water to make 1-3/4 cups total. Return mixture to saucepan. Add buttermilk, sugar, butter, and salt. Heat or cool as necessary to 120 to 130 degrees.*
- *In a large bowl, combine 2 cups of the flour and dry yeast. Add the potato mixture. Beat with electric mixer on low to medium speed for 30 seconds, scraping bowl. Beat on high for 3 minutes. Using a spoon, stir in as much of the remaining flour as you can.*
- *On a lightly floured surface, knead, adding more flour if necessary, to make a moderately stiff dough that is smooth and elastic (6 to 8 minutes total). Shape into a ball. Place in a greased bowl, turning once to grease surface. Cover and let rise in a warm place till double (45 to 60 minutes).*

- *Punch down dough. Turn out onto a lightly floured surface. Divide in half. Cover and let rest for 10 minutes. Lightly grease two 8x4-inch loaf pans. Shape each half of dough into a loaf. Lightly dip tops of loaves in a bit of flour. Place in prepared loaf pans with the floured side up. Cover and let rise till nearly double (about 30 minutes).*
- *Bake in a 375-degree oven for 35 to 40 minutes or till done (if necessary, cover with foil the last 15 minutes of baking to prevent over browning). Remove bread from pans and cool on a wire rack.*

- *Alice Kuhar's whole-wheat potato bread variation: Prepare bread as above except reduce all-purpose flour to 4 to 4 1/2 cups and add 2 cups whole-wheat flour, whisking together to combine.*

102 Pão de Queijo: Brazilian Cheese Bread

- Prep: **15 mins**
- Cook: **25 mins**
- Total: **40 mins**
- Servings: **15** servings

Ingredients

- 2 cups whole milk
- Salt (to taste)
- 1/2 cup vegetable oil
- 8 tablespoons butter (melted)
- 4 1/4 cups tapioca flour
- 4 eggs
- 2 cups grated farmer's cheese (or any firm, fresh cow's milk cheese)
- Optional: 1/4 cup cheddar cheese (grated)

190

Directions

- *Gather the ingredients.*
- *Preheat the oven to 350 F.*
- *Mix milk, salt, vegetable oil, and butter in a pot, and bring to a boil. As soon as it boils, remove from heat.*
- *Stir tapioca flour into the milk and butter mixture.*
- *Stir in the eggs and the cheese, and mix well.*
- *Let mixture cool for 15 to 30 minutes so that it will be easier to handle. (You can chill it in the refrigerator for 15 minutes or so)*
- *With floured (tapioca flour) hands, shape the dough into golf ball-size balls and place them on a baking sheet.*
- *Bake rolls for 20 to 25 minutes, until they are puffed up and golden. They will rise slowly and puff up mostly in the last 5 or 10 minutes.*
- *Serve warm.*

103 Jewish Bread Machine Challah

- Prep: **60 mins**
- Cook: **45 mins**
- Rising: **90 mins**
- Total: **3 hrs 15 mins**
- Servings: **16 servings**

Ingredients

- 1 1/2 teaspoons salt
- 1 large egg (beaten)
- 1 large egg yolk (beaten)
- 1 cup water (lukewarm)
- 1/2 cup honey
- 2 1/2 tablespoons oil (vegetable)
- 4 2/3 cups flour (bread)
- 1 1/4 teaspoons yeast (instant or bread machine)
- 1 large egg (beaten for egg wash)
- Optional: sesame or poppy seeds

- *Add salt, egg, egg yolk, water, honey, and oil to the bread pan. Spoon flour on top of the liquid. Add yeast.*
- *Select the Basic/White or Sweet cycle and the Light Crust setting and press Start.*
- *At the start of the final rise, press Pause. Remove dough from bread pan, transfer to a floured surface and punch down gently.*
- *Divide dough into thirds. Roll each third into a 10-inch long rope. Lay the three ropes out parallel to each other on a floured surface so they are very close, but not touching. Braid ropes together snugly. Tuck ends under to form an oblong loaf.*
- *Brush braid with beaten egg and sprinkle with sesame or poppy seeds, if desired, pressing the seeds into the dough.*
- *Remove kneading paddle(s) from bread pan. Place braid in pan and press Start to continue the cycle.*
- *The machine will tell you when the bread is done. Remove to a wire rack to cool completely before slicing.*

Common Bread-Making Issues

Bread making problems appear all the time. Once you've been baking for a while and gained experience, you can often tell if the dough is right by how it responds to touch and how it feels, or even by just looking at it. But, in the beginning, when things don't work out, it can be quite complicated to figure out what went wrong.

Of course, these problems can be solved quite simply, and we all know how much the experience gives us – but this is the age of information, so before having to encounter all of the results caused by such problems, you can just let me fill you in on some of them and advise you how to avoid them:

*Problem one: **My dough isn't rising.***

Solution: A lot of people think the dough won't rise unless they leave it somewhere really warm for several hours. In reality, you don't need anything special for the dough to rise. I always use instant yeast as it is more reliable, then normal cold water. If it doesn't grow, it might be because of the yeast – fresh yeast can be weak. Also, if you use water that is too hot or add certain acidic ingredients and certain spices like pepper and lemon powder, it can kill your yeast.

*Problem two: **I feel I need to increase my dough's rise.***

Solution: You don't need an exquisite proving drawer to get a good result, generally, if you want to boost, you can just warm it up a little bit. Water that's around 35°C will give the dough an instant boost. You can even pop the dough in a cold oven and put a reading lamp or something similar above it – the heat from the bulb can give it a nice boost. You can also try adding an extra pinch of sugar as it will give the yeast more to feed on.

Problem three: **My finished loaf is kinda heavy and soggy.**

Solution: **There are actually a few things that can cause this, but it mainly happens because of the way in which the bread has been baked. I often recommend people to go and buy a cheap, marble cutting board to use as a baking stone. These boards usually come in the perfect size, so you can avoid buying an expensive baking stone.**

Preheat it in the oven, at the 460-500 °F, shape your loaf on a piece of non-stick paper, and then, when it's proved, carefully put it straight onto the hot stone and lower the temperature of the oven down to 180-200°C. Most loaves turn out soggy at the bottom because they haven't got the required heat, but this is how you can simulate that.

Problem four: **When I'm kneading the dough, it sticks to the work surface and my hands.**

Solution: **The solution strictly depends on what bread you're making. Things like, for example, focaccia have a runny dough that makes it bubbly.**

A normal loaf becomes less gluey the more you knead it - at first, the dough is always wet and sticky, but once you've kneaded it for five to six minutes, it becomes less so and becomes glossy as it develops a coat, which is the gluten forming. After a couple more minutes of kneading, you will get to a point where your hands become cleaner through the kneading motion, as the dough isn't sticky anymore. If it seems, like reaching this point is taking too long, just give it another sprinkle of flour.

Problem five: *I feel like my dough has over proved, but I can't really tell.*

Solution: **There is not one, but a couple of things that can cause over proving. Usually, it happens because the yeast sat for too long. It may not necessarily be exhausted, but the air bubbles could become too big, or it may have lost its structure. Generally, if you leave it to prove for over 40 minutes, it goes into an over proved state, which won't give you a good loaf. If you want to prevent that, don't let the dough double – once it has grown by roughly two thirds, it's already good to go in the oven as it will continue growing in there, and you will get what's called the 'oven spring.' One working way to tell whether your dough has proved enough or not is by pressing it with your finger. It should have a spring back feedback and return to its shape quickly, but not too much - if it springs back really quickly, it probably means that it started to overprove and has taken too much air inside.**

Problem six: **My free-form/formless loaf rises bakes unevenly.**

Solution: **You want to create a skin on your loaf to stop this from happening. If you were making, for example, a round loaf of bread, you need to put some flour on your hands, tip out your proved dough, and then do kind of a tucking and spinning action, so you're continually rotating the dough and tucking it under itself. In the process, it will start to develop a really tight skin, becoming almost like a nice tight football. The fact you have created that surface tension will give you a perfectly even bake.**

Problem seven: **My baked bread falls apart when I cut it.**

Solution: **Firstly, it the reason might be you used too much wholewheat flour, as you didn't add enough regular white flour for creating the gluten, which gives it a texture. Not enough water and too much flour can cause crumbly bread. It's a common mistake - people often add more flour if the dough is too sticky rather than kneading through it.**

Problem eight: **My crust is thin and flimsy.**

Solution: **A crust is actually pretty tough to achieve at home because it appears from baking in a really good, airtight, hot oven.**

That's why store-bought factory bread is so crusty - they have such ovens, and they can throw water in to create that blast of steam for a good crust. Some people try to put a tray filled with water at the bottom of the oven, but domestic ovens are mostly not airtight enough to hold that steam in place and let it do something.

Problem nine: **My sourdough starter has died.**

Solution: **These starters die all the time, and it's usually because they've been forgotten about and sat for too long. They have a short shelf life, and they're quite hard to bring back as starters are living creatures with live bacteria. If it's gone pink, moldy, or red, the best thing to do is get rid of it as it's most likely too far gone.**

Problem ten: **My loaf just cracked during baking.**

Solution: **When you put the dough in the oven, it expands, but you want to control that. Slightly slashing the loaf horizontally or diagonally cuts through the surface and will encourage it to grow in the specified direction.**

Using the list above, you can determine what went wrong with your fresh-baked bread and fix that next time.

The last advice is: change the ingredients as necessary, make sure you always add what you need, and if you make changes to the recipe, aim to keep the right proportions. That's all there is to it.

CPSIA information can be obtained
at www.ICGtesting.com
Printed in the USA
BVHW050937060221
599512BV00013B/1921